Critical Guides to French Texts

C000162978

68 Laclos: Les Liaisons dangereuses

Critical Guides to French Texts

EDITED BY ROGER LITTLE, WOLFGANG VAN EMDEN, DAVID WILLIAM

LACLOS

Les Liaisons dangereuses

Second edition

Simon Davies

Reader in French
The Queen's University of Belfast

Grant & Cutler Ltd
1998

© Grant & Cutler Ltd 1998
ISBN 0 7293 0409 4

First edition 1987
Second edition 1998

DEPÓSITO LEGAL: V. 4.021 - 1998

Printed in Spain by Artes Gráficas Soler, S.A., Valencia for
GRANT & CUTLER LTD
55-57 GREAT MARLBOROUGH STREET, LONDON W1V 2AY

Contents

For Anne

Prefatory Note

As is customary when dealing with *Les Liaisons dangereuses*, references throughout will be to individual letters so that any edition may be used. Italicized numbers in parentheses, followed by page references, refer to numbered items in the Bibliography at the end of this volume.

For invaluable advice and suggestions I am indebted to Peter Broome and Tim Unwin.

1. Introduction

Les Liaisons dangereuses is an epistolary novel which is concerned with deception and self-deception in high society. It is a tale of love and death which unfolds in just over five months. The action takes place almost exclusively indoors, either in Paris or in a country-house. External nature plays no role in this late eighteenth-century text. In a complex network of relationships, the main characters reveal varying degrees of gullibility and/or duplicity. At the end of the drama, the five major participants leave the stage. Tourvel and Valmont die, Merteuil flees to Holland, Cécile enters a convent, and Danceny joins the Order of Malta. They are all exiled from the *monde*. In an age of sociability, they are socially dead.

The author of the novel, Pierre-Ambroise-François Choderlos de Laclos was born in Amiens in 1741, the second son of a family belonging to the minor nobility. In 1761 he became a lieutenant in the army, a profession he was to follow for most of his life. Over the next fifteen years or so, he moved around France from garrison to garrison and obtained a few promotions. At the same time he was writing and publishing some verse. With Saint-Georges supplying the music, he adapted Mme Riccoboni's novel *Ernestine* for the stage as a comic opera. This was performed for the one and only time in July 1777 at the Comédie Italienne. It was not a success and the adaptation has unfortunately been lost.[1] Undaunted by this setback, Laclos probably set to work on *Les Liaisons dangereuses* when stationed in Besançon in 1778. Certainly, the following year, while supervising fortifications on the island of Aix, he was busy composing his novel. On leave in 1780, he spent the first six

---

[1] It is possible that other works may have disappeared too. Angus Martin has edited a short story, *Histoire de Pauline*, which may have been composed by Laclos, in his *Anthologie du conte en France 1750-1799* (Paris, Union Générale d'Editions, 1981), pp.349-63. Letters by Laclos are still being discovered from time to time.

months of the year in Paris, again labouring on his manuscript.

In December 1781, he was granted a *permission tacite* by the authorities to bring out his novel. On 16 March 1782 he signed a contract for a first edition of 2,000 copies. He was to be paid 1,600 *livres* (one recalls that Cécile has 'soixante mille livres de rente'). The novel was published between 7 April and 10 April. Marie-Antoinette and Beaumarchais both acquired this first edition which sold so well that Laclos signed a second contract for a reprint on 21 April. In correspondence about the novel, Mme Riccoboni informed Laclos: 'Tout Paris s'empresse à vous lire, tout Paris s'entretient de vous. Si c'est un bonheur d'occuper les habitants de cette immense capitale, jouissez de ce plaisir' (*1*, p.759). It was clearly a best-seller and at least a further fourteen editions appeared that year.

Either towards the end of 1782 or the beginning of 1783, Laclos met Marie-Soulange Duperré in La Rochelle. She bore him a son in 1784 and they married two years later. During this period he had not, however, been idle on the literary front. In 1783 he had begun work on a 'Discours' about the education of women, before embarking on a treatise entitled *Des femmes et de leur éducation*. His preoccupation with contemporary literature is evident from the number of allusions and quotations inserted in *Les Liaisons dangereuses*. In the *Mercure de France* of 1784 he reviewed a translation of Fanny Burney's *Cecilia*. He praised the novel and ranked it 'parmi les meilleurs ouvrages de ce genre, en exceptant toutefois *Clarisse*, celui des romans où il y a le plus de génie; *Tom Jones*, le roman le mieux fait; et *La Nouvelle Héloïse*, le plus beau des ouvrages produits sous le titre de roman' (*1*, p.469). This hit-parade of novels is interesting if not surprising. The epistolary novels of Richardson and Rousseau enjoyed immense prestige and influence in France as the text of *Les Liaisons dangereuses* and Laurent Versini's annotations bear ample witness (*1*, pp.1163-411). Fielding, who did not enjoy as great a vogue as his compatriot in France, is here commended for producing a finely structured work, a clear indication of Laclos's concern with artistry and technique.

In the years leading up to the Revolution we find Laclos composing works as diverse as the *Lettre à Messieurs de l'Académie française sur l'Eloge de Vauban* (1786) and a *Projet de numérotage des rues de Paris* (1787). During the Revolution Laclos was quite active, though the precise nature of his involvement at various times is still shrouded in uncertainty. What is certain is that he entered the service of the Duc d'Orléans as a secretary and spent time with his employer in London in late 1789 and early 1790. He drafted political pamphlets and joined the Club des Jacobins in October 1790. In 1791 he retired from the army but joined again the following year. In 1793 he was arrested in March, freed in May, and re-arrested in November. With the execution of his protectors, the Duc d'Orléans and Danton, it is obvious from the first letter he wrote from prison to his wife that he anticipated a similar fate. He sent her some locks of his hair as a keepsake: 'C'est un petit monument de tendresse que je te prie de conserver' (*1*, p.793).

Be that as it may, he escaped the guillotine and was set free in December 1794 to return to his beloved family. In just under five years he was back in the army and taking part in a number of campaigns. We read in a letter of April 1801 that he was considering writing a second novel which would illustrate the contention that 'il n'existe de bonheur que dans la famille' (*1*, p.1064). It was a project that he never carried out. Laclos was to die from illness and exhaustion during a posting in Italy in September 1803.

2. Characterization

In *Les Liaisons dangereuses* Laclos provides us with a series of portraits which offer varying degrees of the particular and the general. In his correspondence with Mme Riccoboni, he links his depiction of Merteuil to the tradition of the *caractère*, the character as type. Using Molière's Tartuffe as an example, he states that the latter was not based on one man but was an amalgam: 'cet homme n'existait pas; mais vingt, mais cent hypocrites avaient commis séparément de semblables horreurs: Molière les réunit sur un seul d'entre eux, et le livra à l'indignation publique' (*1*, p.761). Furthermore there is nothing exclusively French about Merteuil; on the contrary, women with 'des sens actifs et un cœur incapable d'amour; quelque esprit et une âme vile' (*1*, p.762) could be found anywhere with only 'des différences locales'. Laclos is claiming to create types of universal applicability who will strike the reader through their moral attributes and will not be particularized through quirks of dress or physical features.

In the Vicomte de Valmont, Laclos creates the character of a young bachelor who is endowed with wit, charm and social graces. Apparently without financial cares, or parental constraints or responsibilities, he lives and acts as a free agent. He moves in the ambit of a society whose fundamental validity he neither questions nor rejects. When we meet him he is an experienced and accepted member of 'la bonne compagnie' whose membership he enjoys, notwithstanding his unsavoury reputation, through his inherited position and worldly etiquette. His life is devoted to the fulfilment of egotistic pleasures, 'toujours des femmes à avoir ou à perdre' (LXXVI). Educated, intelligent, Valmont embodies the principles of a man determined to enjoy the here and now while planning the immediate future to his advantage. Since he harbours no religious 'prejudices' or moral scruples, Valmont is very much the *libertin*, a character common in eighteenth-century fiction. Colonel Morden in Richardson's *Clarissa* offers a valuable definition to the eponymous heroine:

> A libertine, my dear cousin, a *plotting*, an *intriguing* libertine, must be generally remorseless — unjust he must always be. The noble rule of doing to others what he would have done to himself, is the first rule he breaks; and every day he breaks it; the oftener, the greater his triumph [...] To be a libertine at *setting out*, all compunction, all humanity must be overcome. To *continue* to be a libertine, is to continue to be everything vile and inhuman. Prayer, tears, and the most abject submission are but fuel to his pride. (Vol.2, letter LXXIV)

At the time this novel was written, *libertinage* had sloughed off most of its seventeenth-century connotation of philosophical free-thought to imply primarily licence in sexual matters. Nevertheless, Laclos has Valmont write of sex in a manner which suggests the latter's ideas are underpinned by a mechanistic and sensationalist philosophy. He claims that for many women 'le plaisir est toujours le plaisir; et n'est jamais que cela'. Male partners are merely 'des facteurs, de simples commissionnaires' among whom 'celui qui fait le plus est toujours celui qui fait le mieux' (CXXXIII). For Valmont, sex without ethical impediment does not amount to an absence of self-restraint. On the contrary, he prizes above all self-mastery, the capacity to eliminate chance from everyday existence, to impose order on the disorder of life. He is not a womanizer chasing any available female as easy conquests are beneath his dignity. He is not out to set records in some sexual Olympics: for him it is quality, not quantity, that counts. If he requires sexual gratification, he turns to a whore (Emilie), whereas it is a woman who presents a seemingly insuperable challenge (Tourvel), who whets his appetite and sets off a calculated campaign of seduction. He is preoccupied by his *gloire*, a cynical devaluation of an aristocratic ideal. His is a mock enactment of Pierre Corneille's line: 'A vaincre sans péril, on triomphe sans gloire'

(*Le Cid*, II, 2). Unlike the knights of old he will attack women, not defend them.

By selecting Tourvel as the target of his attentions, Valmont is able to decipher her glances and gestures as signals of the effect he has on her; seduction follows deduction (VI, XXI, XXIII, CXXV). Through a form of *explication de texte*, he pierces the surface messages of Tourvel's letters to discover her state of mind and emotional turmoil. He sets himself up as the rival to God: 'j'oserai la ravir au Dieu même qu'elle adore' and 'Je serai vraiment le Dieu qu'elle aura préféré' (VI). The technique pays off as the 'jolie prêcheuse' (XXIII) is impressed with the moral and religious progress of his rehabilitation, a case of actions speaking louder than words! However, he has succeeded almost too well, for in the ensuing interview emotions take over and he all but gains an untimely victory. This would have removed the pleasures and satisfactions of the planned campaign:

> Quelle est donc notre faiblesse? quel est l'empire des circonstances, si moi-même, oubliant mes projets, j'ai risqué de perdre, par un triomphe prématuré, le charme des longs combats et les détails d'une pénible défaite; si, séduit par un désir de jeune homme, j'ai pensé exposer le vainqueur de Madame de Tourvel à ne recueillir, pour fruit de ses travaux, que l'insipide avantage d'avoir eu une femme de plus! Ah! qu'elle se rende, mais qu'elle combatte; que, sans avoir la force de vaincre, elle ait celle de résister; qu'elle savoure à loisir le sentiment de sa faiblesse, et soit contrainte d'avouer sa défaite. (XXIII)

As for the hunter, the chase and anticipation are the paramount pleasure, not the conquest. His English predecessor, Richardson's Lovelace, utters similar sentiments: 'more truly delightful to me the seduction progress than the crowning act' (*Clarissa*, Vol.2, letter XCIV). Tourvel becomes more cautious after this incident and attempts the conventional remedy of avoiding communication with Valmont. The 'timide dévote' returns his letter unopened, an action Valmont terms with characteristic wit a 'ruse diabolique' (XXXIV). She is expecting a letter from her husband, who is on business in Dijon. Valmont therefore contrives to have his letter franked from that town. In a rather theatrical scene, he relishes her distress when she unseals it (XXXIV). He still acts the respectful admirer and begs an interview with her (XLII). He extols the joys of reciprocal love and blames society for corrupting him as a callow youth:

> Qu'ai-je fait, après tout, que ne pas résister au tourbillon dans lequel j'avais été jeté? Entré dans le monde, jeune et sans expérience; passé pour ainsi dire, de mains en mains, par une foule de femmes, qui toutes se hâtent de prévenir par leur facilité une reflexion qu'elles sentent devoir leur être défavorable; était-ce donc à moi de donner l'exemple d'une résistance qu'on ne m'opposait point? ou devais-je me punir d'un moment d'erreur, et que souvent on avait provoqué, par une constance à coup sûr inutile, et dans laquelle on n'aurait vu qu'un ridicule? (LII)

He pretends that he was really 'délicat et sensible' and she has shown him the error of his ways: 'C'est en vous voyant que je me suis éclairé: bientôt j'ai reconnu que le charme de l'amour tenait aux qualités de l'âme' (LII). Such are her exceptional powers that she has transformed his existence and won his undying devotion: 'Vous connaître sans vous aimer, vous aimer sans être constant, sont tous deux également impossible' (LXVIII). Through acumen and scheming he becomes convinced of her love, though he admits to Merteuil that he fears that Tourvel may escape him (LXXVI). The obstacles that she places in his path are a challenge and a source of exquisite anticipation as he recognizes that, after her fall the 'femme céleste' will just be an ordinary mortal (XCVI).

In an interview with Tourvel, he feels that he has gained 'le consentement de l'âme', but recognizes such consent has not, as yet, 'passé jusqu'aux sens' (XCIX). A sudden reversal, however, puts him in disarray. With surprising candour, he tells Merteuil of his perplexity over Tourvel's unexpected departure. In Valmont's eyes Tourvel is 'perfide' and her conduct is inexplicable (C) (des Grieux reacts in similar manner towards

Manon in the abbé Prévost's novel). The master analyst of female behaviour has been outsmarted, and can merely exclaim 'O femmes, femmes!' in a style akin to the opening of Figaro's famous monologue (Beaumarchais, *Le Mariage de Figaro*, V, 3).[2] Tourvel is a more resolute opponent than he believed, though her escape arouses his vengeful wrath. The setback prompts Valmont to re-assess his situation just as misfortune had done for des Grieux in *Manon Lescaut*. He ponders on the problems that he has himself generated and Laclos accords him a world-weariness which has often been overlooked:

> Mais quelle fatalité m'attache à cette femme? cent autres ne désirent-elles pas mes soins? ne s'empresseront-elles pas d'y répondre? quand même aucune ne vaudrait celle-ci, l'attrait de la variété, le charme des nouvelles conquêtes, l'éclat de leur nombre, n'offrent-ils pas des plaisirs assez doux? Pourquoi courir après celui qui nous fuit, et négliger ceux qui se présentent? Ah! pourquoi?... Je l'ignore, mais je l'éprouve fortement. (C)

Here adversity creates self-doubt and Valmont must continue his quest for Tourvel in order to banish anxieties about his chosen role in society. His happiness, his peace of mind can be restored only by the possession of Tourvel. In practice, he is depicted as anything but a self-contained character with this need of other people to confirm the image that he wishes to project. Indeed, the very act of writing this letter (C) appears to be a therapeutic exercise as he tries to reassure himself that he is still, like Merteuil, a superior being.

Laclos then has Valmont resort to using Azolan as a spy on Tourvel's conduct. The servant intercepts her letters, pumps her maid for information and is guaranteed his master's protection, should the need arise (CI). Valmont is portrayed as being short on invention, since he does not want to repeat known tricks

---

[2] René Pomeau suggests that Beaumarchais may have borrowed a line from Laclos's novel. In letter XXXVIII Merteuil exclaims: 'que ces gens d'esprit sont bêtes!' The first scene of *Le Mariage de Figaro* contains Suzanne's declaration 'Que les gens d'esprit sont bêtes!'; this provokes Figaro's retort 'On le dit' (*2*, p.318, note).

which would not redound to his credit and '[se] traîner servilement sur la trace des autres, et triompher sans gloire!' (CX). The feigned illness routine nevertheless reaches Tourvel's notice through Mme de Rosemonde's letters. Eventually he manages to arrange a meeting with the Présidente through the intervention of Père Anselme. The delicately modulated tones of Valmont's letter convince the priest of his contrition and Père Anselme intercedes to set up the stage for Tourvel's downfall (CXX, CXXIII). The seduction is recounted at length and culminates in the telling admission by Valmont of the exceptional nature of the experience: 'L'ivresse fut complète et réciproque; et, pour la première fois, la mienne survécut au plaisir. Je ne sortis de ses bras que pour tomber à ses genoux, pour lui jurer un amour éternel; et, il faut tout avouer, je pensais ce que je disais. Enfin, même, après nous être séparés, son idée ne me quittait point, et j'ai eu besoin de me travailler pour m'en distraire' (CXXV).

Here he has evidently lost self-control, his emotions have been naturally expressed, not artificially restrained. (Previously, in letter LVII, Valmont had recounted how he had been conquered by his own role-playing: 'J'ai tant dit [à Danceny] que l'amour honnête était le bien suprême [...] que j'étais moi-même, dans ce moment, amoureux et timide'.) His genuine affection for the Présidente has been apparent for some time (e.g. XLIV, XCIX, C). When he informs Merteuil that the Présidente had given him back 'les charmantes illusions de la jeunesse' (VI), the sentiments were truer than he supposed. He has become, in Laurent Versini's words, a 'libertin surpris par l'amour' (*29*, p.614). Yet his *libertin* ideal will not permit him to yield to his feelings and he ends the letter (CXXV) with the demand for the 'récompense' of a renewed relationship with Merteuil. He deftly sidesteps the *péripétie* of the traffic jam (CXXXV) and regains Tourvel's confidence (CXXXIX). Valmont then delivers what will be the killer blow by sending his mistress a letter dictated by Merteuil: 'je l'ai copié tout simplement, et tout simplement encore je l'ai envoyé à la céleste Présidente' (CXLII). The Marquise can therefore savour her triumph not just over her rival, Tourvel, but also over Valmont's deep attachment to her.

Hubris has caused Valmont to put aside his genuine feelings and fall into Merteuil's trap.

His parallel seduction of Cécile is small beer by comparison. She is an ignorant lass, unworthy of his attention, even to please Merteuil. Nevertheless, things change when her mother, the 'infernale mégère' (XLIV), endeavours to thwart his progress with Tourvel. At that juncture, vengeance is called for. Merteuil contributes by getting Cécile under Rosemonde's roof and he duly seduces the girl. He betrays her trust and the friendship with Danceny, in whose interests he is supposedly acting. He has, however, captured only Cécile's 'personne' and not her 'cœur' as Merteuil points out (CXIII). To heighten the joy of his revenge, he takes no contraceptive measures. In pedagogical guise, he further depraves his pupil by instructing her in a 'catéchisme de débauche', and derives perverse pleasure from hearing sexual terms repeated from such ingenuous lips. In a significant aside he confides: 'je ne sais pourquoi, il n'y a plus que les choses bizarres qui me plaisent' (CX). Is this indicative of a jaded appetite, an aspect of his life which he normally tries to conceal from himself? At any rate he will claim to be greatly amused at Cécile's pregnancy (one wonders whether the time-scale is too short for him to acquire such knowledge?). Later he evidences no compassion at all when she miscarries (CXV, CXL). Cécile is no more than a minor diversion while he seeks to land the major prize of Tourvel.

Throughout the work Valmont avails himself of opportunities for sexual indulgence when a challenge is involved. A night with Emilie is all the sweeter since it is at her Dutch partner's expense. The Dutchman is endowed with a comic French accent, ever the misfortune of ridiculous foreigners, duped and intoxicated, then deprived of his pleasure with Emilie for the sport of Valmont (XLVII). The aristocrat gets the better of the stupid bourgeois, just as old M. de G... M... is duped in *Manon Lescaut*. Stimulated by the difficulties presented by the presence of Vressac, her current lover, Valmont manages nevertheless to spend the night with the Vicomtesse de M... . He then goes on to save her from embarrassment when she is locked out of her room and ends up by winning the gratitude of the reinstated lover (LXXI) — a splendid piece of entertainment straight out of a medieval *fabliau*!

However, the ultimate test of Valmont's powers is the conquest of Merteuil. He may capture Tourvel's heart, Cécile's senses, but the Marquise's mind is another matter — his triple goal is more demanding than Prévan's triumph over the three 'inséparables'. There is no possibility here of the dupery that he employed in his relations with Tourvel, Cécile and Danceny. His exchanges with Merteuil take place between ostensible equals who are in fact rivals. As they consider themselves the supreme connoisseurs of the game of life, they seek each other's admiration and plaudits. Valmont's aim is to convince the Marquise that he is holding steadfastly to a cold, calculated *libertin* code of seduction and that Tourvel is an object worthy of conquest. The bantering tone of the opening of his first letter to Merteuil displays the irony and humour which pervades most of their correspondence: 'Vos ordres sont charmants; votre façon de les donner est plus aimable encore; vous feriez chérir le despotisme' (IV). The missive ends with a provocative put-down: 'J'ai dans ce moment un sentiment de reconnaissance pour les femmes faciles, qui m'amène naturellement à vos pieds'. He teases Merteuil with the threat that Prévan is out to subdue her. He then demonstrates his narrative talents when he recounts the tale of the latter's audacious victory over the three 'inséparables' (LXX, LXXIX).

In an effort to minimize her skill in outwitting Prévan, Valmont accords Merteuil simply grudging acknowledgement (XCVI). The fact that they now communicate only by letter seems to be sapping the foundations of their relationship: 'Tant que j'étais auprès de vous, nous n'avions jamais qu'un même sentiment, une même façon de voir; et parce que, depuis près de trois mois, je ne vous vois plus, nous ne sommes plus de même avis sur rien' (CXV). Even the seduction of Tourvel fails to renew a sexual relationship with Merteuil, thus widening the rift between them. Valmont is pushed to the limits of endurance by Merteuil's evasive tactics. He reminds her that they both possess sufficient material to destroy each other, and that he must either be her lover or her enemy (CLIII). Such an either/or ultimatum does not bring Merteuil to heel and Valmont cannot achieve this final act of domination.

The break with Merteuil provokes the revelation of his treachery to Danceny. When mortally wounded by Danceny in a duel, Valmont dies with dignity. It is the honourable death of a nobleman. It is neither the ignominious exit of a scoundrel nor is it marked by the tortured ravings of a sinner. He had tried to set himself up as God in assuming the mantle of Providence organizing the lives of those around him. Unlike the characters of Crébillon *fils*, nothing for Valmont must be the outcome of chance: 'mais pouvais-je souffrir qu'une femme fût perdue pour moi, sans l'être par moi! Et devais-je, comme le commun des hommes, me laisser maîtriser par les circonstances?' (LXXI). Laclos portrays him as yearning to transcend the arbitrary discontinuity of human relations and impose his own design. Ultimately he is doomed to fail, and indeed some readers have seen his death as tantamount to suicide. The novelist could be viewed as implying that the real world is inimical to any ideal and that his creature's *gageure* has been lost. Would it be unreasonable to suggest that the author could have made a self-disciplined Valmont overcome an impetuous and angry Danceny?

Laclos presents the Marquise de Merteuil as a young widow living in a male-dominated society. Sexually liberated she may be, but in secret, for in the world she cultivates a reputation for strict virtue. Whereas Valmont may enjoy his renown as a lecher and still be admitted in society, she must defer to conventional morality to maintain membership of the *cercle*. To fulfil her ambitions, she has to acquire even greater skill than Valmont in manipulating people to her advantage. Accordingly, her powers of observation and artistry must be finely honed.

In common with Valmont, she possesses many insights into human motivation and practice. Her most striking observations frequently concern women and love. In a manner prefiguring Stendhal's theory of *cristallisation*, Laclos has her declare: 'ce charme qu'on croit trouver dans les autres, c'est en nous qu'il existe; et c'est l'amour seul qui embellit tant l'objet aimé'

(CXXXIV). Women tend to credit often unworthy men with 'perfections chimériques' which have been created solely by their own imagination (CIV). She writes dismissively of the 'femmes à délire et qui se disent à *sentiment*' who are incapable of reflection and 'confondent sans cesse l'amour et l'amant: qui, dans leur folle illusion, croient que celui-là seul avec qui elles ont cherché le plaisir en est l'unique dépositaire; et vraies superstitieuses, ont pour le prêtre le respect et la foi qui n'est dû qu'à la divinité' (LXXXI). She holds that love is like medecine, '*seulement l'art d'aider à la nature*' (X).

With regard to sex, she claims in a rather deterministic way that pleasure is the 'unique mobile de la réunion' of couples, but it cannot cement relationships and neither can anyone choose to be in love: 'de l'amour, en a-t-on quand on veut?' (CXXXI). In terms recalling Marceline in *Le Mariage de Figaro* (I,4) she chides Danceny: 'Vous autres hommes, vous n'avez pas d'idées de ce qu'est la vertu, et de ce qu'il en coûte pour la sacrifier! Mais pour peu qu'une femme raisonne, elle doit savoir qu'indépendamment de la faute qu'elle commet, une faiblesse est pour elle le plus grand des malheurs' (CXXI). Elsewhere (CXIII) Valmont is given a lesson on the attitudes and roles of ageing women as a corrective to his simplistic pronouncements. She takes women between the ages of forty and fifty as social types and divides them into two categories: 'La plus nombreuse, celle des femmes qui n'ont eu pour elles que leur figure et leur jeunesse, tombe dans une imbécile apathie, et n'en sort plus que pour le jeu et pour quelques pratiques de dévotion; celle-là est toujours ennuyeuse, souvent grondeuse, quelquefois un peu tracassière, mais rarement méchante' while the other, much smaller group is 'celle des femmes qui, ayant eu un caractère et n'ayant pas négligé de nourrir leur raison, savent se créer une existence, quand celle de la nature leur manque, et prennent le parti de mettre à leur esprit les parures qu'elles employaient avant pour leur figure. Celles-ci ont pour l'ordinaire le jugement très sain, et l'esprit à la fois solide, gai et gracieux'.

These social perceptions and insights into human motivation are derived from a careful process of self-education. In letter LXXXI, she provides Valmont with a potted autobiography which purports to demonstrate her superior genius. Valmont, like all men, has had it easy compared to her and women in general. She has, therefore, planned her activities to restore the balance, has devised techniques unknown before her, regarding herself as being born to 'venger mon sexe et maîtriser le vôtre'. (Despite this claim, hers is a personal liberation as she is happy to abuse her fellow women.) Everything she has done has had an ulterior motive, and she should not be confused with the ordinary members of her own sex. The principles to which she adheres are of her own invention, not unthinkingly borrowed from others, and she boasts of being 'mon ouvrage'. She relates a common theme of eighteenth-century fiction, namely the entry of a young person into the world. In her case, however, the apprenticeship is extremely unusual. Unlike Cécile and Tourvel, she was not educated in a convent. Finding herself arbitrarily 'vouée par état au silence et à l'inaction', she claims, from the age of fourteen, to have had the capacity for detached observation and to have cultivated the art of deceit. She tolerates her husband of an arranged marriage by using him merely as a sexual initiator. Through boredom while in residence at his 'triste campagne' she daringly admits sexual relations with some virile locals: 'ne m'y trouvant entourée que des gens dont la distance avec moi me mettait à l'abri de tout soupçon, j'en profitai pour donner un champ plus vaste à mes expériences'. It was there that she learnt that love is only an excuse for sexual gratification: 'l'amour que l'on nous vante comme la cause de nos plaisirs n'en est au plus que le prétexte'. Her early widowhood, therefore, afforded her the perfect opportunity to exercise freedom in selecting her own life-style.

To buttress her first-hand knowledge of society, she turned to books during her token period of mourning. She read philosophers, *moralistes* and novelists. She learnt much and particularly appreciated the novelists for teaching her social customs. *Ennui* being the greatest bugbear—she later complained to Valmont: 'je m'ennuie à périr' (CXIII)—she yearned to reappear in society to try out her theories. She is capable of combining 'l'esprit d'un auteur' with 'le talent d'un comédien' and is proud of building up a false image of herself in society as the incarnation of virtue. No-one is able to pierce her mask and she manipulates her secret lovers into discretion. Her relationship with Valmont was initiated on account of his reputation. She admits he was special, hence the present confidences: 'vous manquiez à ma gloire; je brûlais de vous combattre corps à corps'. Indeed, he was 'le seul de mes goûts qui ait jamais pris un moment d'empire sur moi'. Since they were in fact in love, 'nous nous aimions, car je crois que c'était de l'amour' (CXXXI), the fight resulted in a physical and intellectual draw. They parted as equals, each in a position to discredit the other. When she sets out to obtain total victory over the impertinent Prévan, it is in line with her dictum: 'Il faut vaincre ou périr'. In a transposition of traditional sexual usage, she boasts: 'je veux l'avoir et je l'aurai' (cf.XX 'si vous n'avez pas cette femme, les autres rougiront de vous avoir eu').

In the course of this, the longest letter in the work, Merteuil states that she never writes self-incriminating letters. One is thus entitled to ask why she is doing so here. The answer is that the author wants to show her blowing her own trumpet, seeking to overwhelm Valmont with her brilliance. He is aware of her guile and sexual expertise, and is now being asked to admire the ingenuity of her training programme. In fact the whole of her correspondence to Valmont is geared to dominating him and forcing him to acknowledge her supremacy. As a parodic version of the chivalrous knight, he must serve her interests, show his obeisance and bring her his trophies (II, XX, CVI). His deeds will be worthy of publication, but it is she who will take charge of his memoirs (II). She rouses his jealousy by tormenting him with accounts of the varied pleasures that she has granted the undeserving Belleroche: 'Après le souper, tour à tour enfant et raisonnable, folâtre et sensible, quelquefois même libertine, je me plaisais à le considérer comme un sultan au milieu de son sérail, dont j'étais tour à tour les favorites différentes. En effet, ses hommages réitérés, quoique toujours reçus par la même femme, le furent toujours par une maîtresse nouvelle' (X). She goads him by asserting that even the inexperienced Danceny 'pourrait, malgré ses vingt ans, travailler plus efficacement que vous à mon bonheur et à mes plaisirs'

(CXXVII). She observes that experiencing jealousy is unworthy of a *libertin* as it signifies loss of self-mastery: 'vous êtes jaloux, et la jalousie ne raisonne pas' (CLII).

Ironically, Merteuil becomes jealous herself. She is jealous of Valmont's attachment to the Présidente: 'je n'ai pas oublié que cette femme était ma rivale, que vous l'aviez trouvée un moment préférable à moi, et qu'enfin, vous m'aviez placée au-dessous d'elle' (CXLV,cf.CXXVII, CXXXIV). She cannot stomach the thought that any woman may excel her, and her response is singularly lacking in cool detachment. In fact, one must be wary of thinking that Merteuil is invariably accurate in her perceptions and in control of her actions. Her dismissive summary of Tourvel as being irredeemably '*encroûtée*' and an undignified '*espèce*' does not accord with the reality of the Présidente's personality as the novel unfolds (V). Nevertheless, she does succeed in inveigling Valmont into breaking his relationship with Tourvel, and then refuses to offer herself as the requested prize. It is she who will declare open warfare destroying initially their partnership and subsequently their lives (CLIII).

If she battles to attain overt control over Valmont, her attempts to control others take place in covert operations. Mme de Volanges, Danceny, and Cécile are all unaware they are being manipulated by her. For mother and daughter, she is the paragon of solicitous virtue. The former receives letters of exemplary uprightness, while the latter is enraptured to be accorded her counsel and assistance (e.g. LXXXVII, XXIX). Danceny, poor mite, will eventually share her generous endowments in blind ignorance of her purpose. She is amused not just at the prospect of the success of her stratagems but also delights in advance at the prospect of the discomfiture of her victims. Once she has spilt the beans about Cécile's correspondence with Danceny to Mme de Volanges, Merteuil enjoys firing the young girl's expectations: 'Je m'amusais à lui monter la tête sur le plaisir qu'elle aurait à le voir le lendemain; il n'est sorte de folies que je ne lui aie fait dire. Il fallait bien lui rendre en espérance ce que je lui ôtais en réalité' (LXIII). Her purpose in proposing to outmanœuvre Prévan is not merely to avenge his presumption but also to bring some amusement into the vegetative existence of the past six weeks by promising herself a 'gaieté' (LXXIV). To devastate Belleroche by abruptly severing their relations is an exquisite thought: 'rien ne m'amuse comme un désespoir amoureux. Il m'appellerait perfide, et ce mot de perfide m'a toujours fait plaisir; c'est, après celui de cruelle, le plus doux à l'oreille d'une femme' (V).

Merteuil is portrayed as possessing a controlled sexuality. This she indulges in a variety of roles to dominate her lovers. Moreover, there are a number of hints at her sensual response to Cécile's young charms: 'si j'avais moins de mœurs, je crois que [Belleroche] aurait, dans ce moment, un rival dangereux; c'est la petite Volanges. Je raffole de cet enfant: c'est une vraie passion' (XX, cf.XXXVIII, LXIII). Are these lesbian innuendoes inserted to imply that Merteuil can brook no sexual restraints? Is it possible to infer that, like Valmont, only 'choses bizarres' may in future tempt her jaded palate?

One thing is certain, towards the end of the work Merteuil is depicted as less and less in control. One detects a certain nostalgia when she harks back to her affair with Valmont. She acknowledges that the time cannot be recaptured when she was 'heureuse' (CXXXI). She enquires whether Valmont has forgotten that he made her 'heureuse, parfaitement heureuse' (CXXXIV). Merteuil's world is finally torn asunder when her correspondence is divulged and the infamous letters LXXXI and LXXXV are circulated in Paris. She loses her lawsuit, is declared bankrupt and snubbed in that most worldly of places, the theatre. Physical retribution is exacted through her contraction of smallpox, and her consequent disfigurement is emblematic of her moral corruption. She is forced to flee to Holland. Doubtless Laclos wishes us to infer that such an exile would be a living death for a socialite. Indeed she can be considered as having been punished more severely than Valmont. Merteuil is presented as failing because she placed too great a confidence in her own abilities.

The Présidente de Tourvel is twenty-two years old and belongs to the *noblesse de robe*, a group basically assimilated into the

older aristocracy in the late eighteenth century. It is significant
that Merteuil, in running her down, makes no mention of any
inferior social status (V). Tourvel's marriage had been arranged
by Mme de Volanges and the young wife cares dutifully for her
husband and is outwardly content with her lot.[3] Otherwise she
has no particular responsibilities to engage her attention. She
has no children of her own, nor does she have to look after any
ageing relatives. She appears to follow religious ethics and
practice more through a sense of conformity than through any
deep experience or conviction. Religion plays no more part in
her initial refusal of Valmont than it does in Mme de Clèves's
refusal of Nemours in Mme de Lafayette's novel. Nevertheless,
her austerity is renowned and presents a challenge to Valmont.
Superficially there would seem to be nothing remarkable about
her. She seeks no prominence and is by no means a centre of
attention, claiming, as she does, that she possesses 'peu de
gaieté' (XLV).

Valmont, on the other hand, accords her a 'gaieté naïve et
franche'. He contradicts Merteuil's assessment of her appearance: 'toute parure lui nuit; tout ce qui la cache la dépare: c'est
dans l'abandon du négligé qu'elle est vraiment ravissante. Grâce
aux chaleurs accablantes que nous éprouvons, un déshabillé de
simple toile me laisse voir sa taille ronde et souple. Une seule
mousseline couvre sa gorge; et mes regards furtifs, mais
pénétrants, en ont déjà saisi les formes enchanteresses' (VI). The
simplicity of her attire and the freedom of her movements
attract Valmont by their freshness and lack of sophistication.
She has something in common with the natural woman
described in Laclos's treatise *Des femmes et de leur éducation* (*1*,
pp.402-03), but her veneer of social etiquette and convent
upbringing preclude too close an identification. She has a fund
of 'sensibilité' which Valmont aims to develop and

---

[3] Tourvel's situation brings to mind the real-life advice proffered by Chesterfield
to his son. In a letter composed in French, Chesterfield writes: 'on m'assure que
Madame de Blot, sans avoir des traits, est jolie comme un cœur, et que
nonobstant cela, elle s'en est tenue jusqu'ici scrupuleusement à son mari, qu'il y
ait déjà plus d'un an qu'elle est mariée. Elle n'y pense pas; il faut décrotter cette
femme-là', *The Letters of Philip Dormer Stanhope, Earl of Chesterfield*, edited
by John Bradshaw, Letter CLXVI, vol.I (London, Swann Sonnenschein, 1905),
pp.427-28.

exploit (VI). As an 'âme sensible' she dislikes the idea of animals being hunted (XXI). She admits that the account of Valmont's charity to the peasants '[l'] a attendrie jusqu'aux larmes' (XXII). She is so moved by this action of Valmont that she almost succumbs in a subsequent encounter (XXIII).

Far from being an actress, she has not the knack of hiding her reactions, and is unable to refrain from blushing (VI, XXXIV). She is incapable of a 'regard menteur' and cannot 'couvrir le vide d'une phrase par un sourire étudié'. Nor, for that matter, is she vain, for although she has 'les plus belles dents du monde, elle ne rit que de ce qui l'amuse' (VI).[4] So great is her emotional turmoil as the result of Valmont's interest that she appeals to him on two occasions 'au nom de Dieu, laissez-moi' (XLIV, XCIX). With a pride equal to Merteuil's, she is horrified at the thought of being placed on a par with the women Valmont has abused in the past. She tells Valmont that it is an 'idée révoltante' to see herself 'confondue avec les femmes que vous méprisez, et traitée aussi légèrement qu'elles' (XXVI), and she takes him to task for such treatment (XLI).

The power of feelings surprises her, and later she can confide in Valmont: 'Je ne vous reproche rien; je sens trop par moi-même combien il est difficile de résister à un sentiment impérieux' (XC). In anguish, she fears the condemnation of public opinion which is 'toujours prompt à mal penser d'autrui' (XLI). She reiterates her anxieties over the loss of her peace of mind: 'cessez de vouloir troubler un cœur à qui la tranquillité est si nécessaire; ne me forcez pas à regretter de vous avoir connu (LVI). She is frightened at the prospect of experiencing the unknown emotion of love. Her reaction to Valmont's apology for love is to foresee its storms and a short-lived happiness followed by regrets and remorse (L). In this letter she informs him with prophetic irony: 'vous feignez de croire que l'amour mène au bonheur; et moi, je suis persuadée qu'il me rendrait malheureuse, que je voudrais n'entendre jamais prononcer

---

[4] Versac, a rakish character of Crébillon *fils*, 'rit le plus souvent qu'il put, pour montrer ses dents', *Les Egarements du cœur et de l'esprit*, édition présentée, établie et annotée par R. Etiemble (Paris, Gallimard, Collection Folio, 1977), p.159.

son nom. Il me semble que d'en parler seulement altère la tranquillité'. She begs Valmont to abandon 'un langage que je ne puis ni ne veux entendre' (LXVII). Merteuil acutely observes that '[Tourvel] épuisera [ses forces] pour la défense du mot, et qu'il ne lui en restera plus pour celle de la chose' (XXXIII). For her, the happiness he advocates is no more than a 'tumulte des sens, un orage des passions dont le spectacle est effrayant, même à le regarder du rivage' (LVI).

All she is ready to accord him is her friendship (LXVII). This is, in reality, a form of self-deception as her much vaunted concern for Valmont's return to the paths of righteousness makes clear. She is supposedly convinced that he is not a 'libertin sans retour' (XI). She pretends that she is carrying out her Christian duty in encouraging him to return to the fold (VIII, XXII). Moreover, she is not above a certain hypocrisy in letters to Mme de Volanges regarding Valmont (XXXVII), and that to a friend who had given her such precise warnings (IX). Insidiously confessing his past sins, Valmont avails himself of this heaven-sent opportunity to proclaim the changes that she has wrought in his character (LII, LVIII). But what a dangerous trap is sincerity when so skilfully abused! In letter XC Tourvel shows her concern for not hurting Valmont and tells him that her absence will not alter her feelings for him. Fearing that familiarity breeds consent, Tourvel, just like the Princesse de Clèves, flees her suitor's presence. Such a flight has saved her 'sagesse', but her 'vertu' has vanished. In the hierarchy of moral values, prudence is clearly inferior to the strength implied by virtue. None the less, the idea of her proselytizing powers betrays her. This notion is fortified by comments from Mme de Rosemonde and Père Anselme with the result that she deludes herself even more (CXXIII, CXIX, CXXIV). The pursuit of Valmont's conversion leads to her seduction.

It is only when her feelings are truly aroused that she can give vent to her sensual responses. Her 'émotion' always left her 'cœur, pour arriver aux sens'. Although her seduction by Valmont had left her in tears, the very next moment Tourvel could experience 'la volupté dans un mot qui répondait à son âme' (CXXXIII). Her 'âme' is fulfilled in providing Valmont with 'bonheur'. Her relationship with Valmont becomes Tourvel's exclusive occupation. She informs Mme de Rosemonde that he is now 'le centre unique de mes pensées, de mes sentiments, de mes actions' (CXXVIII): hers is a total commitment. Her internal harmony has now been restored (CXXXII). She is consumed by the joy of the experience, as is seen in a lyrical letter to the same correspondent. (Laclos does not give us a love letter to Valmont.) She feels a 'bonheur parfait' as the result of her love and can enthuse about Valmont: 'je l'aime avec idolâtrie, et bien moins encore qu'il ne le mérite'. She is completely taken in by him, seeing him as a regenerated man since the start of their sexual liaison: 'depuis qu'il peut se livrer sans contrainte aux mouvements de son cœur, il semble deviner tous les désirs du mien. Qui sait si nous n'étions pas nés l'un pour l'autre! si ce bonheur ne m'était pas réservé, d'être nécessaire au sien!'.

Yet even here a momentary doubt intrudes as she exclaims: 'Ah! si c'est une illusion, que je meure donc avant qu'elle finisse'. Her wish will not be granted. We have already learnt of the physical effects of her emotional disarray after her flight from Valmont (CVII). It is no surprise to discover how rapidly she deteriorates after receiving the devastating letter of rupture. Seeking refuge in a convent does not automatically mean cutting oneself off from the problems caused by the world. The delirious letter which Tourvel dictates to her maid is an eloquent testimony to her confusion (CLXI). The final blow comes when she overhears news of Valmont's demise. This prompts the poignant exclamation that for her he was already dead. In prayer she admits her faults, but begs above all for divine clemency for Valmont. Her end is marked more by regret than remorse; it is the death of the betrayed rather than the adulterous sinner. While all around her weep, Tourvel remains calm and dignified. She is accorded the sort of death conventionally associated with the virtuous rather than the tormented writhings of the wicked (CLXV).

Admirable though many of her qualities may be, it would be a mistake to regard the Présidente as the incarnation of pure innocence. She is enough of a socialite to employ white lies when

it suits her. Just like Mme de Clèves, she feigns minor
indispositions (XXIII, XXV, XL). Valmont notes in
amusement: 'Toute sage qu'elle est, elle a ses petites ruses
comme une autre' (XXV). Indeed, arranging for Valmont's
movements to be watched is not an action beyond reproach.
Whereas reporting that her servant just happened to witness the
scene of 'bienfaisance' is palpably dishonest (XXII). Yet her
greatest lie is to herself, deceiving herself that Valmont would
make the ideal brother she does not possess (XI). She ends up
believing what she wants to believe, as does Guilleragues's
Portuguese nun: 'Qu'on a de peine à se résoudre à soupçonner
longtemps la bonne foi de ceux qu'on aime'.[5] By presenting her
as placing her entire trust in her emotions, unchecked by any
modicum of reason, Laclos portrays her disintegration in a
manner recalling the heroines of Racine.

Cécile is one of a number of teenagers who figure prominently
in major eighteenth-century novels; one thinks of Prévost's
Manon Lescaut or the heroine of Marivaux's *La Vie de
Marianne*. Laclos accords her the first letter in the work which is
brimming with the hopes and expectations of a convent girl
eager to sample the pleasures of the world. She records her
excitement at possessing a desk in which she has the very adult
right to lock up anything she wishes. She will be mingling in the
company of men, and her one thought is of marriage. Her early
letters are full of naïve outpourings, confessing her blunders and
gaucherie in society. For instance, in her panic she mistakes a
cobbler for her future husband (I). In no way has her education
equipped her to cope with the problems of living in a
sophisticated society, and she acknowledges her lack of
composure (III, XIV). Since she is a rather bored adolescent, it
is hardly surprising that she becomes infatuated with the
Chevalier de Danceny.

---

[5] Lavergne de Guilleragues, *Lettres portugaises*, ed. B.Bray and I. Landy-
Houillon (Paris, Garnier-Flammarion, 1983) p.82. Jean-Jacques Rousseau
recognized the same phenomenon: 'On se défend difficilement de croire ce qu'on
désire avec tant d'ardeur', *Les Rêveries du promeneur solitaire*, introduction de
Jean Grenier (Paris, Gallimard, Collection Folio, 1972) p.64.

She does not know what she should or should not do. She responds in a nervous way to Danceny and attempts to justify her conduct to Sophie Carnay: 'On nous recommande tant d'avoir bon cœur! et puis on nous défend de suivre ce qu'il inspire, quand c'est pour un homme!' (XVI). Sophie replies as the voice of innocent caution, but Cécile counters: 'Mais quel mal peut-il y avoir à écrire, surtout quand c'est pour empêcher quelqu'un d'être malheureux?' (XVIII). In the same letter, Cécile ingenuously asserts that no girl could possibly have found herself in a predicament similar to hers. All they had shared in the convent were but childish games compared to the raptures of love: 'Mais l'amour, ah! l'amour!...un mot, un regard, seulement de le savoir là, eh bien! c'est le bonheur' (LV). Elsewhere she asks Merteuil: 'on m'a bien dit que c'était mal d'aimer quelqu'un; mais pourquoi cela?' (XXVII). Here is a question which stresses the seeming contradiction that the natural, spontaneous feeling of love is to be suppressed in favour of the artificial convention of marriage.

Cécile has no capacity or authority to organize her own life. She has to rely on her maid to tell her when she should dress (I). After Merteuil's interference, she has to yield Danceny's letters to her mother (LXI). Later on she will submit to Valmont's exhortation to obtain the key of her room. Her principal problem is that she has no-one in whom she can confide, who will offer her sound advice and act in her interests. Sophie is too inexperienced, while her own mother operates double standards (XXVII). Indeed, Mme de Volanges has no intimate contact with her daughter. After the night of Cécile's deflowering, Valmont notes the mother's discomfiture: 'Et pour la première fois, sa mère, alarmée de ce changement extrême, lui témoignait un intérêt assez tendre!' (XCVI). It is not Mme de Volanges but Merteuil who informs Cécile of the marriage plans (XXIX). It is Merteuil who offers Cécile books to aid her behaviour in society (XXIX). Merteuil is her 'bien bonne amie' who allows the girl to write to her, since Cécile finds writing less embarrassing than conversation (XXVII).

It is consequently understandable why the Marquise makes such an impression (XXXIX, LV), and, like some malevolent agony aunt, ensnares Cécile in her vengeful schemes. The relationship with Danceny is encouraged by Merteuil who also undermines Mme de Volanges's reputation in order to increase her hold on her 'pupil'. Once under her domination, Cécile may be treated with scorn and any possibility of her self-esteem may be removed. Cécile has admitted her inability to compose letters (XVIII) and Merteuil devastates her on this score: 'Vous écrivez toujours comme un enfant. Je vois bien d'où cela vient; c'est que vous dites tout ce que vous pensez [...]. Vous voyez bien que quand vous écrivez à quelqu'un, c'est pour lui et non pas pour vous: vous devez donc moins chercher à lui dire ce que vous pensez, que ce qui lui plaît davantage' (CV). She proves easy sport for Valmont who dishonours her to exact vengeance on her mother (LXVI). Not only does she lose her virginity, but Valmont discredits her mother in a concerted effort to deprave (CX). He delights in taking charge of her correspondence. He dictates a letter addressed to Danceny in which he sings his own praises with stupendous irony: 'Oh! vous avez là un bien bon ami, je vous assure! Il fait tout comme vous feriez vous-même' (CXVII).

Her pregnancy and miscarriage further confirms her ignorance of the facts of life. Cécile is endowed with what Merteuil defines as a 'fausseté naturelle' which is allied to considerable sensuality. She is 'naturellement très caressante' and 'sa petite tête se monte avec une facilité incroyable; et elle est alors d'autant plus plaisante, qu'elle ne sait rien, absolument rien, de ce qu'elle désire tant de savoir' (XXXVIII). Merteuil claims that never was anyone more liable to 'une surprise des sens' (LIV). Cécile is sensually aroused at the thought of Danceny (LV). She is 'toute troublée' when she is seduced by Valmont and almost feels as if she is in love with her initiator (XCVII). She gains physical pleasure from Valmont without emotional involvement (CXIII). Merteuil dismisses her as belonging to 'ces sortes de femmes qui ne sont absolument que des machines à plaisir' (CVI). Her affair with Valmont leads her to deceive Danceny (CIX). She never acquires the ability to assess her circumstances with detachment or maturity. Valmont can quite accurately maintain that '[Cécile] ne perd pas son temps à réfléchir!' (CXL). When her whole world comes crashing down, she can, like Tourvel, seek asylum only in a convent as an escape from the demoralizing experience of the world. Throughout the novel, Cécile does not really act, but rather is acted upon. So great are her innocence and her ignorance that, despite her sexual initiation, the fifteen-year-old has not matured emotionally. She lacks what Valmont terms 'consistance' (CXXIX). One may therefore feel that she fails to achieve the dignity of the victim attained by Tourvel.

Danceny, like Prévost's des Grieux, is a prospective Chevalier de Malte. He has not, despite Cécile's fears (VII), pronounced final monastic vows, and is still technically on the marriage market (LI). He is from a good family, employs servants, but is not wealthy. At the outset of the work, he can be envisaged as the male counterpart of Cécile with his limited experience matching hers. Like Cécile, he is also taxed by Valmont with a lack of 'consistance' (CLI). However, being a man, he enjoys more freedom of action. He is the ideal beau to distract Cécile and rescue her from boredom (VII). He uses his talents as a musician to spend time with Cécile in a way comparable to Almaviva's ruse with Rosine in Beaumarchais's *Le Barbier de Séville* (III,4). Once smitten with her virginal charms, he pursues her with engaging honesty and clumsy sincerity. On a par with one of Marivaux's characters, the impact of genuine attraction causes him to lose his internal harmony: 'Sans vous je serais encore, non pas heureux, mais tranquille. Je vous ai vue; le repos a fui loin de moi, et mon bonheur est incertain' (XVII, cf.XXVIII). In a series of letters he manifests both his devotion and his heartbreak (XLVI, LX). He cannot get the girl out of his mind: 'Lors même que les distractions du monde m'emportaient loin de vous, je n'en étais point séparé. Au spectacle, je cherchais à deviner ce qui vous aurait plu; un concert me rappelait vos talents et nos si douces occupations. Dans le cercle, comme aux promenades, je saisissais la plus légère ressemblance. Je vous comparais à tout; partout vous aviez l'avantage' (LXXX).

When Mme de Volanges has been informed of the

surreptitious relationship, he writes her a respectful letter explaining his behaviour and stressing the sincere nature of his feelings: 'Un vil séducteur peut plier ses projets aux circonstances, et calculer avec les événements: mais l'amour qui m'anime ne me permet que deux sentiments: le courage et la constance.' (LXIV). Nevertheless, despite his awareness of this type of sexual predator, he is blind to Valmont and his machinations. (It is perhaps surprising that he seems ignorant of Valmont's reputation.) For him Valmont is an 'ami fidèle et sûr' (LX) who merits Cécile's complete trust and whose requests should be carried out (LXV, XCIII). Ironically, Danceny becomes an accomplice to Cécile's seduction. He pressurizes her into consenting to Valmont's plan to obtain a duplicate key to her room (although he is blissfully unaware of the object involved).

Increasingly he is treated as a puppet in the bitter struggle between Valmont and Merteuil. The Marquise praises him to discountenance her adversary and claims he has a 'goût très vif' for her (CXIII). Besotted with Merteuil, he tells Cécile: 'Quel bonheur de vivre uniquement pour vous deux, de passer sans cesse des délices de l'amour aux douceurs de l'amitié, d'y consacrer toute mon existence, d'être en quelque sorte le point de réunion de votre attachement réciproque' (CXVI). Cécile is unable to discern the reasons behind Danceny's extravagant praise, and the point has now been reached where each of the young lovers is keeping a secret from the other. Danceny has forsaken his role of authentic 'amant' for that of an 'homme à bonnes fortunes' (CLV). In addition, he offers a dubious justification for his infidelity with Merteuil when he claims his heart remains with Cécile (CLVII).

When Merteuil has apprised him of Valmont's treachery, although he remains oblivious of her part in it, he is galvanized into righteous indignation and nobly slays the Vicomte. Once he is in receipt of the Valmont-Merteuil correspondence and discovers all, he blackens the Marquise's reputation by circulating letters LXXXI and LXXXV in Paris. Finally, he passes on this correspondence and his own with Cécile (one remembers that Mme de Volanges had returned his letters) to

Mme de Rosemonde, and abandons a society which had so savagely abused him. At the start of the novel, he was presented as a decent young man. Through being easily influenced, he contributed to his own misfortune and to that of the girl he held most dear.

Cécile's mother could be regarded as contributing to *Les Liaisons dangereuses* less through what she does do, than what she does not do. Laclos shows her neglecting her daughter's welfare, allowing her to make a fool of herself by falling asleep in company (III). Later on she does not have the slightest inkling of her offspring's seduction by Valmont or its consequences. She notes that Cécile is consumed by a 'mélancolie dangereuse'. This sorry state she attributes to the 'malheureuse passion' for Danceny and tells Merteuil with unintended irony: 'j'aime mieux compromettre mon autorité que sa vertu'. She mistakes the cause of Cécile's distress and contemplates breaking off the engagement to Gercourt. Her remarks about arranged marriages would have won the approval of Diderot or Marivaux: 'Ces mariages qu'on calcule au lieu de les assortir, qu'on appelle de convenance, et où tout se convient en effet, hors les goûts et les caractères, ne sont-ils pas la source la plus féconde de ces éclats scandaleux qui deviennent tous les jours plus fréquents?' (XCVIII). Her sympathetic advocacy of a marriage of inclination is countered by Merteuil's display of stern virtue (the Marquise fears that her revenge on Gercourt may be thwarted). Mme de Volanges is portrayed as dithering about her daughter's prospective husband, and is accordingly easy prey to Merteuil's eloquent manipulation (CIV). Moreover, in her request for advice from Merteuil, she makes the astonishing admission that she would like the time to 'étudier ma fille que je ne connais pas' (XCVIII). Here is surely implicit evidence of Laclos's concern about the inadequate education of women which he was to examine in his treatises.[6] Right to the end of the work, Volanges remains ignorant of the events which have befallen her daughter. Although Volanges may be judged to be amiss in her

---

[6] Jean Bloch provides an assessment of this aspect of his work in 'Laclos and women's education', *French Studies*, XXXVIII (1984), 144-59.

abdication of the role of maternal counsellor to Cécile, she does, nevertheless, offer sensible warnings to Tourvel. It is she who composes an accurate picture of Valmont:

> Encore plus faux et dangereux qu'il n'est aimable et séduisant, jamais depuis sa plus grande jeunesse, il n'a fait un pas ou dit une parole sans avoir un projet et jamais il n'eut un projet qui ne fût malhonnête ou criminel [...] sa conduite est le résultat de ses principes. Il sait calculer tout ce qu'un homme peut se permettre d'horreurs sans se compromettre; et pour être cruel et méchant sans danger, il a choisi les femmes pour victimes. (IX)

Volanges confesses that it is inconsistent to admit such a 'liaison dangereuse' as Valmont into society. However, with his family name and great wealth, he early recognized that 'pour avoir l'empire dans la société, il suffisait de manier, avec une égale adresse, la louange et le ridicule' (XXXII). She is aware that people do not respect him but are too frightened to incur his displeasure and subsequent hostility. Tourvel does not heed her warning, and avows on her deathbed: 'Je meurs pour ne vous avoir pas crue' (CXLVII). In one of the many ironies of the book, Mme de Volanges had contributed to Tourvel's downfall by suggesting the idea of having Valmont followed (IX). Unwittingly, she had furnished him with the opportunity to stage the scene of spurious *bienfaisance*.

Yet, as her remarks about Valmont show, Mme de Volanges is far from being a simpleton. She may have no idea of the real reasons which prompted her daughter's request to take the veil, but she does talk sense on this subject. She is anxious to save Cécile from 'les tourments et les dangers d'une vocation illusoire et passagère' because 'souvent on se croit appelée à Dieu, par cela seul qu'on se sent révoltée contre les hommes' (CLXXIII, cf. CLXX). Here she is passing remarks analogous to those propagated by the *philosophes* (e.g. Diderot, *Jacques le fataliste*, *3*, p.700). It is Volanges who reports much of the dénouement of the novel. Her letters to Mme de Rosemonde record her impotence during the decline of Tourvel, and include a touching account of their mutual friend's death. She ponders on the ways of destiny which have wrought havoc on Tourvel who had seemed so happy and well-placed just a year ago, and has now been destroyed by a single piece of imprudence. In a manner akin to Zadig, the bemused hero of Voltaire's tale, she exclaims: 'O Providence! sans doute il faut adorer tes décrets; mais combien ils sont incompréhensibles!' (CLXV). In the same letter, she wonders about the current value attached to feelings, having witnessed her daughter's distress: 'Cette sensibilité si active est, sans doute, une qualité louable; mais combien tout ce qu'on voit chaque jour nous apprend à la craindre'. After having misinterpreted the cause of Cécile's dejection, she also fails to appreciate that it is unguided 'sensibilité' which is at issue here.

Elsewhere she relishes imparting a juicy item of gossip when she informs Rosemonde of an eye-witness account of Merteuil's public humiliation in the theatre — if only she were not related to her — and also of Prévan's triumphant rehabilitation (CLXXIII). The rueful comments of the mother in the concluding letter of the work form a poignant contrast with the cheerful babble of the daughter in the first: 'j'éprouve en ce moment que notre raison, déjà si insuffisante pour prévenir nos malheurs, l'est encore davantage pour nous en consoler' (CLXXV). It is appropriate that she should end the work as she has been one of the most unifying as well as one of the most duped characters.

Mme de Rosemonde is a venerable octogenarian who exhibits a vitality which belies her advanced years (VIII). It is in her country home that much of the action takes place. While certainly upset at the deaths of Valmont and Tourvel, her material situation is hardly affected by the events of the novel. Now past the age of passion, and seemingly confined to her home, she acts as both spectator and commentator, drawing on her vast store of experience. (She is in the tradition of the elderly sage, and has something in common with the *vieillard* whom Bernardin de Saint-Pierre was to portray in 1788 in *Paul et Virginie*.) She intervenes predominantly late in the work as a sympathetic confidante to Tourvel, and eventually as the recipient of the gathered correspondence from Danceny. As a counsellor to Tourvel she is wise yet ineffectual, her physical difficulty in writing perhaps paralleling her impotence at influencing events. Without being told, she realizes Tourvel's attachment is to Valmont. As evidence of his awareness of time passing, Laclos has her note that 'je me suis rappelé que c'est encore comme au temps passé' (CIII). In this letter she is sensitive to Tourvel's emotional problems, and recognizes her 'daughter's' need to share them. She informs her of Valmont's 'religious' progress (CXIX) and of his melancholy state. She is glad Tourvel cannot see him because his condition would inspire 'cette tendre pitié qui est un des plus dangereux pièges de l'amour' (CXXII). Ironically, she contributes to Tourvel's downfall through commenting on her nephew's supposed indisposition (CXII, CXXII), thereby eliciting the worried responses of Tourvel which Valmont intercepts (CXV). When she is told of the Présidente's submission to Valmont, she advises her in a kindly, motherly fashion, pointing out the dangers attending her situation.

She analyses at length the differences between male and female attitudes to love. Although men may experience the same 'ivresse', they do not know 'cet empressement inquiet, cette sollicitude délicate, qui produit en nous ces soins tendres et continus, et dont l'unique but est toujours l'objet aimé'. Men enjoy the happiness they experience, while women enjoy the happiness they create. It is this difference, so essential but little noticed, which 'influe pourtant, d'une manière bien sensible, sur la totalité de leur conduite respective. Le plaisir de l'un est de satisfaire des désirs, celui de l'autre est surtout de les faire naître. Plaire n'est pour lui qu'un moyen de succès; tandis que pour elle, c'est le succès lui-même' (CXXX). Rosemonde is here celebrating the superiority of the woman in love relationships where her feelings are genuine and she wishes to give rather than to take. Men can get away with a lot more in the eyes of public opinion which distinguishes between 'inconstance' and 'infidélité'. In the eighteenth century 'inconstance' implied a lover abandoning someone to whom he was not really already attached, while 'infidélité' meant deceiving one's mistress with another woman — the latter was more acceptable in the rake's code as Versini notes (*1*, p.1340, note 2). These reflections are designed to aid Tourvel in counteracting the 'idées chimériques d'un bonheur parfait dont l'amour ne manque jamais d'abuser notre imagination' (CXXX).

Notwithstanding their wisdom, these observations do no more to save Tourvel than Mme de Volanges's strictures on Valmont. Her advice will, however, be followed by Volanges in permitting her daughter to enter a convent. Here Rosemonde discreetly refrains from telling her friend of the grounds for this course of action (CLXXII). While recognizing that Danceny has some room for complaint, Rosemonde nevertheless makes clear to him his share of responsibility in Cécile's misfortune. In no uncertain manner he is told: 'celui qui le premier tente de séduire un cœur encore honnête et simple se rend par là même le premier fauteur de sa corruption, et doit être à jamais comptable des excès et des égarements qui la suivent' (CLXXI). Danceny is the one who first caused Cécile to resort to dishonesty, and thus became her first 'liaison dangereuse'. Yet Rosemonde has a self-confessed weakness for Valmont who was to be her heir, enjoys her nephew's lively company, and cannot therefore be viewed as a paragon of virtue. Despite his faults, to lose Valmont in a duel — in common with enlightened thinkers, she abhors this practice — is a blight on her last years.

A few comments may be helpful on some of the minor characters who serve to flesh out the social background of the novel. In certain respects, Prévan could be envisaged as a Valmont lookalike, an almost equally successful rake. Despite his comeuppance at Merteuil's hands, Prévan's rehabilitation at the end of the work says much for the morality of the aristocratic world created by Laclos. Gercourt's personality must be judged, not just from the respectful letter to Mme de Volanges,[7] but also from his previous abandonment of Merteuil.

[7] I do not agree with Laurent Versini who speaks of the 'sot Gercourt, dont les clichés et le respect des convenances font un gendre sur mesure pour Mme de Volanges' (*1*, p.1334). Gercourt seems to me to have drafted the sort of letter which will appeal to his future mother-in-law.

The Maréchale de *** and the 'dévote voisine' are included to suggest a society eager for scandal. Since the organization of aristocratic life is often labour-intensive, servants are depicted playing a significant, if unobtrusive role. Azolan is Valmont's willing accomplice and is given a certain individuality when Laclos stresses his snobbish indignation at the prospect of donning 'une livrée de robe après avoir eu l'honneur d'être chasseur de Monsieur' (CVII). Unlike Azolan, who has much in common with his counterparts in traditional comedy, Bertrand is a character more suited to the sentimental *drame bourgeois*. The author has him asserting his dignity by claiming that 'dans tous les états, on a un cœur et de la sensibilité' (CLXIII).

What Laclos offers us in *Les Liaisons dangereuses* is a gallery of portraits, especially on the distaff side. Cécile is the young girl; Tourvel, the young wife; Merteuil, the young widow; Volanges, the middle-aged mother; and Rosemonde, the old lady. On the male side we are presented with Danceny, the young man; Valmont, the experienced rake; and Azolan, the impertinent servant. The eighteenth-century reader was well used to these representative types, these descendants of La Bruyère's *caractères*. As Versini reminds us in reference to Valmont, the 'scélérat méthodique' is 'autant qu'un type social, un type littéraire, que Laclos trouvait au moins ébauché dans ses lectures' (*1*, p.1145). However, one may feel that the author has achieved more than representative types in his major characters, that they are indeed particularized. Merteuil, who, for example, generalizes disparagingly about the 'femmes à prétentions' (LXXXI) and '*gens à principes*' (LXXXV), is depicted in her revolt as trying to escape such reductionist classification. In the course of the novel few characters evolve, or achieve a heightened awareness of themselves, of others and the world around them. The two exceptions are Valmont and Tourvel. Unless one questions the authenticity of his attachment to Tourvel, and some readers do, the impact of the Présidente attacks the very foundations of his principles. Inwardly he may have found them wanting. Tourvel, on the other hand, after the anguish of self-doubt, finds momentary fulfilment in her commitment to Valmont, the unutterable joy of a new experience. One could apply to her Tennyson's lines from 'In Memoriam':

> Tis better to have loved and lost
> Than never to have loved at all.

3. The Letter-Novel

The novel in the eighteenth century was in the process of establishing itself as a major form of creative expression. Unsanctioned by antiquity, it sought to prove its worth by the moral utility and the claims to truth so often asserted in the prefaces. To demonstrate that a work justified the attentions of a serious reader, the latter had to be, or pretend to be, convinced that the text was an authentic account of lived experience.[8] In approximately the first half of the eighteenth century, this consideration led to the popularity of the *mémoire* form. A character recalled his or her earlier life, often from the vantage point of retirement, and with differing amounts of retrospective commentary. Amongst the drawbacks of this format are the unilateral point of view and a lack of suspense. Partly to overcome these disadvantages, the late eighteenth century in France saw an increasing vogue for epistolary fiction. Here one must bear in mind that it was a century of great letter-writers. For the polished members of high society, armed with their quill pens, the art of letter-writing was, like that of conversation, one of the social graces.

The eighteenth-century reader was quite used to letters being mentioned, or even inserted in fiction. (Private letters of Voltaire or Rousseau were often reproduced in the periodicals of the day.) In *La Princesse de Clèves* (1678), Mme de la Fayette's heroine is distressed by a letter that she wrongly attributes to M. de Nemours. Both *La Vie de Marianne* and *Manon Lescaut* contain letters penned by their heroines which contribute to the development of the plot.

When Laclos came to compose *Les Liaisons dangereuses*, he was exploiting a form which was already a winner. After its success in England, Richardson's *Clarissa* had been translated

[8] Vivienne Mylne offers an excellent discussion of novelistic practice in *19*, pp.1-49.

into French by the abbé Prévost in 1751 and had enjoyed widespread success. Rousseau's *Julie, ou la Nouvelle Héloïse* (1761) was a best-seller which did much to enhance the prestige of the genre as well as the epistolary technique. Although there are examples of letter-novels employing only one correspondent, texts with more than one are commoner and offer increased possibilities. Again the reader is presented with a work which plausibly contains genuine accounts. The reader may experience an almost voyeuristic reaction at being offered something which was supposedly not for 'public consumption'. Various points of view are conveyed and the reader, like a detective, can piece together the jigsaw of evidence as the plot unfolds. The characters act and react before his eyes, the drama is not already over, as is the case with the *mémoire* form.

A letter implies absence, even though an addressee may sometimes be residing in the same house. In other respects, it may be regarded as a substitute for conversation. A carefully wrought letter may be more effective in achieving the writer's ends than a personal meeting, especially when importunate company may be around. Moreover, a letter may not only be read but re-read, and constitutes a material reminder of another person. Acceptance or refusal of a letter are important events which betoken the state of relations between characters. Possession of, or access to, letters often indicates the power of a character. The underprivileged characters usually read the fewest letters.

There are twelve correspondents in *Les Liaisons dangereuses*, which is divided into four parts and contains one hundred and seventy-five letters. The four parts are of roughly equal length but comprise unequal numbers of letters: fifty, thirty-seven, thirty-seven and fifty-one. They also cover unequal periods of time, the first three about a month each, the fourth two and a half months.

The distribution of letters in the novel reflects the importance of various characters in the development of the interlinking plots and sub-plots. Valmont comes out on top as letter-writer with fifty-one, almost a third of the total. Merteuil composes only twenty-eight, but in receiving forty-one she outscores Valmont by four. For the most part the other characters write more letters than they receive, with Mme de Rosemonde being the major exception since she composes nine but is sent twenty-one. The Valmont-Merteuil correspondence occupies over a third of the letters exchanged. Amidst the general interchange of letters between the five main characters Tourvel stands alone: she has no epistolary contact with Merteuil, Cécile, or Danceny.

In Laclos's novel, even when Tourvel resolves not to open them, letters from Valmont reassure her of his continuing interest. She tells Mme de Rosemonde: 'combien je suis peinée de ne plus recevoir ces mêmes lettres, que pourtant je refuserais encore de lire. J'étais sûre au moins qu'il était occupé de moi! et je voyais quelque chose qui venait de lui. Je ne les ouvrais pas, ces lettres, mais je pleurais en les regardant' (CXIV). The presence of a letter would console Danceny: 'si on ne la lit pas, du moins on la regarde' (CL). Cécile longs for the time when she can retain her letters rather than hand them over to Valmont for safe-keeping (LXXXII). For different reasons, Tourvel and Cécile feel the need to re-read letters in their possession (CIX, CXXIV). Possession of letters may suggest involvement, complicity or power. Tourvel sends back Valmont's first letter and requests the return of her own (XXVI). Evidence of Danceny's relationship with her daughter is established when Mme de Volanges discovers letters in the bureau (LXI). To obviate future embarrassments, Volanges demands that the young man return Cécile's correspondence (LXII). Merteuil and Valmont manipulate Cécile's and Danceny's lives through having access to their letters (e.g. LXIV, LXV, LXVI) and even dictating them (CXVII, CLVI). They also attach other people's letters to their correspondence (LX, LXXXVI). As proof of the Présidente's downfall, Merteuil demands written confirmation in the victim's own words: 'on ne reçoit de preuves que par écrit' (XX). Merteuil claims never to have given written testimony of her activities (LXXXI). A note for Belleroche is 'non de mon écriture, suivant ma prudente règle', but penned on her behalf by her servant Victoire (X). Indeed, it is ironic, but fitting, that the release of her correspondence with Valmont by Danceny should have precipitated her disgrace (CLXVIII). The absence of a reply to a letter is a clear indication of the deteriorating relations between Valmont and Merteuil. The Vicomte complains that he has been waiting three days for an answer and that his 'dernière lettre pourtant [lui] paraissait en mériter une' (CXL).

The ability to acquire, even intercept, letters is a necessary talent for the arch-manipulator (CXXV). Valmont suggests that the skill of the pickpocket would not come amiss in the educational programme of the would-be intriguer (XL). The manner of transmitting letters also presents problems. Danceny secretes his first communication to Cécile in the strings of her harp (XVI). When the going gets tough, the young people have to resort to using Valmont as a postman (LXV, LXXVI, LXXX, CLV). Valmont himself has difficulties in making Tourvel receive his letters. He drops one on her bed while she is feigning illness; this she is obliged to accept to avoid scandal (XXV). He uses Azolan as a carrier with a bogus excuse, and elsewhere gives an envelope the appearance of having come from her husband in Dijon (XXXIV); although she rips up this letter in his presence, we learn in letter XLIV that he has obtained it, found it pieced together and stained with her tears.[9]

The skilled letter-writer should always have the addressee in mind. The well-composed letter by no means fits Danceny's definition as being 'le portrait de l'âme' (CL). Merteuil rebukes Cécile with writing like a child, revealing everything and concealing nothing. You are writing for him, not yourself: 'vous devez donc moins chercher à lui dire ce que vous pensez, que ce qui lui plaît davantage' (CV). How blind Cécile is to the fact that here Merteuil is putting her own theory into practice!

To participate in the epistolary exchange is the fictional equivalent of living. Being deprived of writing materials constitutes literary death. Paper, pen and ink are taken from Cécile by her mother (LXIX). This action allows Valmont to become her supplier, which increases her gratitude and dependence (LXXIII). (It also illustrates the ironic theme of the

---

[9] Diderot has the Neveu de Rameau pride himself on his early talents as a seducer: 'A peine entrais-je dans la carrière, que je dédaignai toutes les manières vulgaires de glisser un billet doux' (*3*, p.469).

précaution inutile.) Insignificant characters are given few letters. The author, in his guise as editor, pretends he has suppressed Sophie Carney's correspondence (VII note 1). (The eponymous servant, however, in Tobias Smollett's letter-novel of 1771, *The Expedition of Humphrey Clinker*, has no letter to his credit.)

An additional advantage of the letter-novel over the first-person narration of the memoir format is that, not only is a multiplicity of views made possible, but also different renderings of the identical incident. Valmont can inform Merteuil of his seduction of Cécile (XCVI), while the victim can provide the same correspondent with another version of the event in the next letter. Valmont recounts his scheme to ingratiate himself with Tourvel through a spurious gesture of *bienfaisance* in a village. He relates a tear-jerking scene which is witnessed by Tourvel's 'fidèle espion': 'vous n'imaginez pas quel chœur de bénédictions retentit autour de moi de la part des assistants! Quelles larmes de reconnaissance coulaient des yeux du vieux chef de cette famille' (XXI). This stage-managed incident has the desired effect. Tourvel's servant is taken in and reports Valmont's largesse to his mistress. So impressed is Tourvel that she passes on news of this worthy action to Mme de Volanges (XXII). Later on, we are offered three versions of the traffic jam where Tourvel glimpses Valmont and Emilie ensconced in a carriage (CXXXV, CXXXVII, CXXXVIII). In each case the reader is in the privileged position of possessing all the interpretations or misinterpretations of the same event.

Letters do not merely recount past events in narrative form, they also contain verbatim accounts of conversations at often implausible lengths. Here we encounter the convention of total recall which is utilized to give more weight to significant exchanges between various characters. (Laclos has to resort to such fictional commonplaces as looking through a keyhole in letter XXIII and eavesdropping in letter LXX.) Valmont frequently reports dialogue in his letters to Merteuil, perhaps indicating his cultivation of a tape-recorder memory as another of his accomplishments! Greater impact is accorded to his important scenes with Tourvel when we relive them through the actual dialogue employed: 'La ferveur de l'aimable prêcheuse me servit mieux que n'aurait pu faire mon adresse. "Quand on est si digne de faire le bien, me dit-elle, en arrêtant sur moi son doux regard: comment passe-t-on sa vie à mal faire? — Je ne mérite, lui répondis-je, ni cet éloge, ni cette censure" ' (XXIII, cf. XL, XCIX, CXXV). Merteuil, on the other hand, reports snippets of conversation, but appears to employ italicized phrases rather than extended dialogue (LXIII, LXXXV). Italics and direct speech are used by Volanges when she reports remarks by the dying Tourvel to Mme de Rosemonde (CXLVII, CXLIX, CLXV). Valmont is able to goad Merteuil further when he quotes Prévan's boasting and adroit dupery in accurate terms (LXX, LXXIX). The status of Azolan is enhanced by Valmont's citing his very words to Merteuil, an indication, perhaps, of the increasing importance of the lower classes in late eighteenth-century fiction (XLIV). All in all, actual speech and dialogue recorded in this manner help to mingle time sequences, adding variety and vitality to the relation of the tale.

A recurrent technique in *Les Liaisons dangereuses* is the italicized insertion of terms which have appeared in previous correspondence. Most of the characters indulge in this practice to a greater or lesser extent. Merteuil is fond of picking out phrases from Valmont's letters with a view to undermining his self-esteem. Sometimes it is to taunt him over his delusions about his relationship with the Présidente: *'les illusions de la jeunesse'* (X), *'ce charme inconnu'* (CXXVII), *'une femme étonnante, une femme délicate et sensible'* (CXXXIV). At other times it is to show her superior understanding of general matters (LXXXI, CXIII). Valmont, on the other hand, remembers Merteuil's false claim about her 'petite maison' (X) when she told Belleroche: 'Je ne l'ai eue que pour vous'. In letter CLV he tells Danceny that his assignation will be in a 'petite maison délicieuse, *et qu'on n'a prise que pour vous'*. Tourvel likewise refers to expressions in Valmont's letters. This demonstrates both her fear of his entreaties and her careful attention to his words: 'Vous convenez vous-même que *ce sentiment est pénible quand l'objet qui l'inspire ne le partage pas'* (LVI, cf. XXVI, L). Meanwhile, Valmont extracts comments from Tourvel's letters which he turns to his own advantage: 'Quel dommage que,

comme vous le dites, je sois *revenu de mes erreurs!*' (LXVIII, cf.
LVIII, CXXXVII). (Here he is treating her as a *belle dame sans
merci*.) The rehearsal of terms by these and the other characters
stresses not just the interrelationship of the letters, but also the
centrality of language as a motive force influencing and creating
the events and atmosphere of the novel.

The distribution of letters in *Les Liaisons dangereuses* is of
consequence in maximizing the effects of this form of fiction.
Laclos was well aware of the advantages to be derived from the
careful placing of letters. Versini has shown how he reordered
the text during his revisions (*29*, pp.290-93). A considerable
degree of monotony can be created by a succession of letters
from the same correspondent to the same addressee. This is a
defect which Laclos may have discovered in Richardson's
Clarissa. There, instead of an interwoven pattern of ideas,
feelings and events, at times one is confronted with something
which is little short of an autobiography.

Laclos, on the other hand, never falls into this trap. True,
there are a couple of examples of Valmont writing successive
letters to Merteuil, but these can be shown to fulfil a particular
purpose. In letter LXX Valmont is warning Merteuil of the
doughty Prévan's plan to outsmart her, whereas in the following
letter, as a counterpoint, he is showing off his skill in duping
Vressac. Letter XCIX depicts Tourvel on the point of surrender,
accordingly placing in stark relief Valmont's consternation, in
the next letter, at her unexpected departure. To keep up the
pressure on Tourvel, two letters are juxtaposed from Valmont
(XXXV, XXXVI), while we already know of the circumstances
surrounding them in a communication to Merteuil (XXXIV). In
order to emphasize her duplicity and growing estrangement,
Laclos has Merteuil, on November 29, tell Valmont that she
does not know the date of her arrival in Paris (CXLV), whilst
informing Danceny she will be there the next day (CXLVI).
Valmont's letters to Tourvel are frequently preceded or followed
by one to Merteuil (e.g. XLVII, XLVIII and CXXXVII,
CXXXVIII) as this juxtaposition not only highlights his ability
to adopt different tones, but also the theory and practice of his
activities. Merteuil is portrayed as prejudicing Cécile against

Gercourt in letter XXXVIII. In the following letter, the Marquise's success in this ploy is illustrated.

The over-use of this cause-and-effect technique would be too mechanical and tedious, so Laclos also employs what one could term, at a pinch, a retrospective device. We learn of Cécile's and Danceny's disarray after Cécile's mother discovers her letters (LIX, LX, LXI), but are ignorant of the reasons which prompted Mme de Volanges's action. If we put them down to chance, we are soon disabused, for in letter LXIII Merteuil informs Valmont that it was she who had betrayed Cécile to her mother. She had pointed out this 'liaison dangereuse' in a well-planned 'chef d'œuvre' the better to control the progress of the young lovers' relationship. Danceny's respectful letter to Mme de Volanges (LXIV) may be viewed in a different light when we note that his following letter to Cécile is sent via Valmont. In a work where most of the letters are brief, usually less than three pages in length, the autobiographical letter LXXXI from Merteuil, in which she displays her precocious talents, is further enhanced by being sandwiched between the juvenile prattlings of Danceny to Cécile and Cécile to Danceny. After Cécile has told her confidante of the seduction by Valmont in letter XCVII, Merteuil is told of Volanges's anxieties about her daughter in the next. The Merteuil advice-centre on a busy day (October 4) counsels virtue to the mother (CIV), vice to the daughter (CV), and taunts Valmont for good measure (CVI). Nevertheless, the supreme example of the placing of a letter must be Mme de Rosemonde's letter CXXVI. There Tourvel is congratulated on the happy turn of events, that 'coup de la Providence', which has saved her. Ironically, Tourvel receives it after her fall; its insertion elsewhere would have been in no way so effective.

The epistolary form suits Laclos's purpose in his presentation of the personalities of Merteuil and Valmont. It allows him opportunities to depict them manipulating other people, showing off to each other and admiring themselves. There is a narcissistic quality to be discerned in the manner in which scenes are relived in their letters. Merteuil boasts about how she amused herself with Belleroche, whereas Valmont pays her in kind by reciting his exploits with Cécile. This erotic pleasure is increased at the thought of a correspondent visualizing particular scenes at second hand, and more exquisitely so if jealousy can be aroused. These letters by no means resemble a *journal intime*: they are not composed for self-exploration, but are written to be read by another or others. In short the epistolary artist wants to be applauded.

4. Art and Technique

The range and register of language employed in the novel are essential ingredients in creating the atmosphere of the fictional world portrayed. It is the polite language of high society, permeated both by fashionable jargon and the vocabulary of sensibility. Despite the nature of his subject-matter, Laclos never resorts to explicit terminology in depicting sexual encounters. Valmont relates his 'réchauffé' with the Vicomtesse de M... by appealing to Merteuil's knowledge of his capacities (LXXI). When Tourvel is finally seduced, we are merely told that she is 'livrée à son heureux vainqueur' (CXXV). Tourvel's maid was presumably naked, but we are informed that hers was 'une toilette que la saison comportait, mais qu'elle n'excusait pas' (XLIV). If Valmont mischievously instructs Cécile in sexual matters using only 'le mot technique' (CX), Laclos does not report the conversation. Talking of Belleroche, Merteuil employs a euphemism, common in eighteenth-century fiction, when she claims that it amuses her to 'le rendre heureux' (XX). Just as in Prévost's *Manon Lescaut*, steamy bedroom scenes are conveyed in almost chaste language. To have made use of vulgar or crude language would have consigned Laclos's novel to the level of the pornography found at that time. *Bienséance* is therefore preserved in language, if not in the conduct described.

As ever, Valmont and Merteuil are revealed as having cultivated the most extensive linguistic competence. They pride themselves on being the masters of the clarity and duplicity of language. Laclos provides Valmont with the right vocabulary in his letters to Tourvel. In the first letter to her, the delicacy of his feelings is feigned by the adoption of *précieux* language: 'prêtez-moi votre raison, puisque vous avez ravi la mienne' (XXIV). In the space of a few lines Valmont is shown appealing to the *femme sensible* with 'figure enchanteresse' and 'sentiment délicieux'; to the _précieuse_ with 'empire' and 'poison dangereux'; and to the _dévote_ with 'j'adorai la vertu' and 'âme céleste' (XXXVI). He can impress her with the elegance of his style in the same letter: 'Sans prétendre à vous obtenir, je m'occupais de vous mériter. En réclamant votre indulgence pour le passé, j'ambitionnai votre suffrage pour l'avenir'. The binary balance of these short sentences exemplifies the careful precision of Laclos's concern with both form and content. Even when dealing with the delicate area of love, he suggests: 'Ce n'est pas que l'aimable franchise, la douce confiance, la sensible amitié, soient sans prix à mes yeux... Mais l'amour! l'amour véritable, et tel que vous l'inspirez, en réunissant tous ces sentiments, en leur donnant plus d'énergie, ne saurait se prêter, comme eux, à cette tranquillité, à cette froideur de l'âme' (LXVIII). This calculated appeal to her _sensibilité_ is reinforced in the same paragraph when he refers to his love being 'le plus tendre' and 'le plus respectueux'. Scheming though Valmont may be, in letter CXXV, Laclos has him pay Tourvel the compliment of a well-wrought account of her seduction. After his opening cry of triumph, he relates in a theatrical manner the scene of her submission, and possibly dignifies it by employing past tenses.

Sensitivity to the subtleties of changing tenses is evident. When Valmont narrates his visit to the destitute family, Laclos has him start with the present tense: 'j'arrive au village; je vois de la rumeur; je m'avance: j'interroge; on me raconte le fait'. Yet when he is moved by their gratitude, there is a switch to the perfect tense: 'mes yeux se sont mouillés de larmes, et j'ai senti en moi un mouvement involontaire, mais délicieux. J'ai été étonné du plaisir' (XXI). The sprightly historic present tense shows him in the self-controlled role of the actor, everything going to plan. Taken unawares, the past tense suggests he is now in the role of spectator, someone who is being acted upon.

In a different vein, the author gives Valmont a pompous, neo-classical style. In letter IV he proclaims that: 'L'amour qui prépare ma couronne hésite lui-même entre le myrte et le laurier' (myrtle being a symbol of love, laurel a token of victory). Whereas in letter XCIX we are offered 'les flèches de l'Amour, comme la lance d'Achille' in remarks about Cécile's ignorance

(Achilles's spear cured the wounds it had inflicted).

However, it is probably Valmont's letter XLVIII which displays the novelist's talents at their best. Here Valmont is depicted as patently proud of his efforts since he sends it to Merteuil under the dubious pretext that he needs to have it 'timbrée de Paris'. In addition to its author, the letter has three readers: Emilie, Merteuil and Tourvel. The first two (plus the novel's real readers) can revel in the ambiguities of Valmont's account. In bed with Emilie, he uses her as a 'pupitre pour écrire à ma belle dévote' (XLVII). The letter is a masterpiece of double meanings, with Tourvel alone unable to comprehend them: 'nuit orageuse', 'agitation d'une ardeur dévorante', 'entier anéantissement de toutes les facultés' etc. Tourvel is led to mistake sexual arousal for emotional turmoil: 'Quoi! ne puis-je donc espérer que vous partagerez quelque jour le trouble que j'éprouve en ce moment?' The exceptional nature of his situation cannot strike her: 'la table même sur laquelle je vous écris, consacrée pour la première fois à cet usage, devient pour moi l'autel sacré de l'amour'. He has to give way to an 'ivresse' and almost apologizes for talking about his 'peine'. The *tour de force* lies not only in the deceit of Tourvel, but in an ironical play on her emotions to arouse sympathy for his sexual indulgence. Valmont can sate his erotic fantasies about Tourvel while simultaneously satisfying his physical appetites with Emilie. Furthermore, when he claims that 'jamais je n'eus tant de plaisir en vous écrivant', it is not just delight at his sexual pleasures and capacity to deceive, but also elation at his literary skill. Merteuil had denigrated his epistolary powers in letter XXXIII, and here he feels he has proved her wrong.

Merteuil is at her best in her correspondence with Valmont. There her letters are characterized by an imperious, mocking tone. She aims to subvert his self-esteem. He is reproached for his ineptitude: 'dès que les circonstances ne se prêtent plus à vos formules d'usage, et qu'il vous faut sortir de la route ordinaire, vous restez court comme un écolier' (CVI). He is chided for his lack of invention: 'je veux encore vous dire que ce moyen de maladie que vous m'annoncez vouloir prendre est bien connu et bien usé' (CXIII). Repeatedly, she emphasizes his unacknowledged love for Tourvel (X, CXXXIV, CXLI).

If Laclos is able to grant Valmont and Merteuil such linguistic expertise, he is equally adept at denying it to Cécile. She often lacks the appropriate expression and her grammar is certainly not of the best. In the following sentence the subjunctive mood is absent in the subordinate clause: 'Je suis bien fâchée que vous êtes encore triste' (XXX). She appears to write as she speaks: 'vous croyez que je vous trompe, et que je vous dis ce qui n'est pas! vous avez là une jolie idée de moi!' and 'A présent que je sais que vous le désirez, est-ce que je refuse de la prendre, cette clef?' (XCIV). Her childish mentality is brought out by her frequent repetitions of the same phrase. This is especially evident in the self-exonerating 'ce n'est pas ma faute' (XVIII, XXX, LXXXII), which even figures in the future tense 'ce ne sera pas ma faute' (XCIV). It is, however, in her sloppy over-use of 'bien' that her inadequacies strike most readers: 'Vous me feriez bien plaisir de me mander si tout cela est vrai. Ce qui est bien sûr, c'est que je ne pouvais pas me retenir de rire; si bien qu'une fois j'ai ri aux éclats, ce qui nous a fait bien peur' (CIX). There are eighteen other appearances of 'bien' in this brief letter to Merteuil; there are eleven in letter XCV and twenty-five in letter XCVII. Laclos was quite conscious of the shortcomings that he accorded Cécile's style as he conferred on Valmont the knack of aping it. The pastiche of her facile turn of phrase is evident in the manner Valmont lards the letters he dictates on her behalf with eight 'bien' in CXVII and nineteen in CLVI.[10]

Danceny is never quite so inept at letter-writing as Cécile, despite the earnest tones of his early missives. It is perhaps more acceptable then that the evolution in his style should mirror the evolution of his conduct. His infatuation with Merteuil is most clearly brought out in the extravagant language employed in his letters. The opening of his first letter shows his fatuousness: 'Si

---

[10] Despite her shortcomings, Cécile's spelling far excels that of the future wife of the *philosophe* Helvétius, who wrote during her convent days: 'Que d'obligations ie vous aye, ma chere maman, de m'avoires ecrit aux jours dhuie [...]. C'est vous ma chere maman, oui c'est votre amitié qui peut me faire suporté toutes les obstacle qui s'opose à mon bonheur. Mon dieu! qu'ils est rude d'aitre malheureux', *Correspondance générale d'Helvétius*, edited by P.Alan, A. Dainard, J. Orsoni and D. Smith (Toronto and Buffalo, University of Toronto Press, 1981), vol.I, letter 72, p.132.

j'en crois mon Almanach, il n'y a, mon adorable amie, que deux jours que vous êtes absente; mais si j'en crois mon cœur, il y a deux siècles' (CXVIII). This hyperbolic language strikes me as not much less preposterous than that of the Arlequins of traditional comedy striving to imitate the precious and gallant vocabulary of the master class. He ends this letter in an equally self-conscious tone: 'Oubliez enfin les *mille raisons* qui vous retiennent où vous êtes, ou apprenez-moi à vivre où vous n'êtes pas'. Six weeks later we find him in exclamatory vein: 'O vous que j'aime! ô toi que j'adore! ô vous qui avez commencé mon bonheur! ô toi qui l'as comblé! Amie sensible, tendre amante, pourquoi le souvenir de ta douleur vient-il troubler le charme que j'éprouve? Ah! Madame, calmez-vous, c'est l'amitié qui vous le demande. O mon amie, sois heureuse, c'est la prière de l'amour' (CXLVIII). Here is the celebration of love fulfilled, of 'amour véritable'. One notes the exultant shifts from formal to familiar address, the caricatured imitation of Rousseauistic outbursts. The language is as bogus as the woman who has roused his passion.

Mme de Rosemonde is also granted a distinctive style as a *grande dame* who has observed society over the years and has the ability to encapsulate her wisdom in a digestible form. In spite of her advanced years, she endures her ailments with good grace and humour. Suffering from a debilitating attack of rheumatism, she is obliged to 'emprunter la main' of her maid to correspond with Tourvel (CXII). She chooses lively, familiar terms to describe her rheumatism as being 'niché cette fois sur le bras droit' with the result that she feels 'manchotte'. Since she is in ignorance of the reasons behind the young girl's fatigue, Rosemonde states that '[Cécile] bâille tant que la journée dure, à avaler ses poings' and 'nous fait l'honneur de s'endormir profondément toutes les après-dînées' (*dîner* meant lunch in the eighteenth century). Her ease of expression and sense of the appropriate lead the ailing woman to portray herself as a 'médecin' counselling Tourvel, whom she takes to be 'convalescent' away from Valmont (CXXVI). She tells her that 'les petites incommodités que vous ressentez à présent, et qui peut-être exigent quelques remèdes, ne sont pourtant rien en comparaison de la maladie effrayante dont voilà la guérison assurée'. The medical vocabulary here, as elsewhere (CXXX), is appropriate from the pen of someone preoccupied with the state of her own health.

Both his insolence and familiarity are brought out in Azolan's chatty letter (CVII). He shows a consummate disregard for Valmont's feelings after Tourvel has bolted (C), when he makes an impertinent aside: 'Mais pourquoi donc est-ce qu'elle s'en est allée comme ça? ça m'étonne, moi! au reste, sûrement que monsieur le sait bien? Et ce ne sont pas mes affaires?' He tends to write as he speaks. However, with a French sense of decorum, Laclos does not allow him the spelling mistakes so often made by servants in English novels (e.g. Joseph Leman in *Clarissa* or Winifred Jenkins in *The Expedition of Humphrey Clinker*). Bertrand, on the other hand, is far more restrained in his expression. He offers almost a pastiche of an *oraison funèbre* of the seventeenth-century preacher, Bossuet, when he proclaims: 'Bon dieu! quand j'ai reçu dans mes bras à sa naissance ce précieux appui d'une maison si illustre, aurais-je pu prévoir que ce serait dans mes bras qu'il expirerait et que j'aurais à pleurer sa mort? Une mort si précoce et si malheureuse!' (CLXIII). The studied tone of his letters matches the solemnity of his task and his respectful sensitivity to Mme de Rosemonde's feelings.

A striking feature of *Les Liaisons dangereuses* which contributes much to the ambience of the work is the use of jargon. No-one could feel truly at ease in 'la bonne compagnie' if he were not conversant with the terminology beloved of socialites and trend-setters. Merteuil captures the tone of this worldly language at the start of a letter to Valmont: 'Ah! fripon, vous me cajolez, de peur que je ne me moque de vous! Allons, je vous fais grâce; vous m'écrivez tant de folies [...] J'en ai pourtant bien ri, et j'étais vraiment fâchée d'être obligée d'en rire toute seule' (XX).

The life-style of *libertins* is clearly suggested at the prospect of 'folies' which enliven the tedium of routine existence. Belleroche will find nothing 'plaisant' if Merteuil and Valmont renew their relationship, but the thought of his discomfiture is certainly 'plaisant' to her. The inexperienced Danceny's conduct with

Cécile is 'beaucoup moins plaisant' than if Valmont had been at work (V). Merteuil employs the same adjective to describe her consolation of mother and daughter (LXIII) and Belleroche's anger after her encounter with Prévan (CXIII). Elsewhere she uses 'plaisant' as a noun when she anticipates Gercourt being, as it were, cuckolded in advance (II). It is selected once more to indicate her feeling of triumph over Valmont when the latter has sent her 'letter' to Tourvel (CXLV). The Vicomte similarly avails himself of 'plaisant' to describe the letter that he wrote to Tourvel while in bed with Emilie (XLVII), and also the idea of stealing the letter or portrait of a rival (continuation of XL). Had it not been for the accidental circumstances, Valmont would have found it 'plaisant' to leave the Vicomtesse in a compromising predicament (LXXI). The same word is employed to evoke Cécile's behaviour the morning after her seduction (XCVI), and later the young girl's repentance after annoying him (CX).

'Gaieté' likewise has acquired a more extensive meaning as that of an amusing action. Merteuil comments in letter LXXIV that it is more than six weeks since she allowed herself a 'gaieté'. The dupery of the Dutchman is called a 'gaieté' when the 'petit tonneau à bière' has become intoxicated with wine (XLVII). Valmont seems to employ even the adjective with a malicious overtone when he declares: 'Le parti le plus difficile, ou le plus gai, est toujours celui que je prends' (LXXI).

Preceded by an indefinite article, 'noirceur' has the concrete sense of a malicious act (VI, CLII). Everything appears to be an 'événement'; Danceny has told Valmont about his 'aventure et le dernier événement' (LIII), while Merteuil wishes to 'accoutumer aux grands événements quelqu'un qu'on destine aux grandes aventures' (LXIII). The Maréchale writes in mock horror at Prévan's attack on Merteuil by asserting 'ces événements-là consolent d'être vieille' (LXXXVI).

Hyperbolic language contributes to the bantering tone. 'Monstre' is a term applied to Valmont by Merteuil (II) and to Prévan by the Maréchale (LXXXVI). The thought of Cécile enjoying Danceny is judged a 'meurtre' (CXIII). Valmont is urged to 'former' Cécile, in other words, to deprive her of her

innocence and conformist prejudices (II). In this same letter
Cécile is not granted the dignity of being referred to as 'elle', but
is dismissed as 'cela n'a que quinze ans' and later 'cela n'a ni
caractère ni principes' (XXXVIII), the neutral term embodying
the would-be superiority of the Marquise. At breakfast,
following her first night with Valmont, Cécile is depicted as an
almost uncoordinated piece of machinery: 'C'était un embarras
dans le maintien! une difficulté dans la marche!' (XCVI).

Adverbs often play a significant role in affected language.
Laclos frequently utilizes 'sérieusement' as a conversational
gambit to introduce sentences (V, X, LXXIV etc.) and even a
letter (CXLV). Euphemisms are words to the wise. In letter II
'sot' implies a cuckold when Merteuil envisages Gercourt's
misfortune. The Marquise writes 'ne finira rien' in letter V when
she claims that Danceny will not progress to the sexual act.
Merteuil is bored with her calm existence, 'ne pouvant
m'occuper', that is having a relationship with someone
(XXXVIII). In what can only be construed as a wink in the
direction of the reader, Laclos has Cécile use '*occupée*' in letter
XXXIX without understanding its full implications. Attention is
often drawn to a word which has acquired an extra meaning
through the use of italics. Damningly, Merteuil talks of Tourvel
as '*encroûtée*'. Just like Diderot's Neveu de Rameau, she
proposes '*espèce*' as a term denying a person any individuality
(V, cf. CXLI). Danceny and Cécile know too little about the
world, and can by no means be considered '*usagé*[s]' (LI, LVII,
CLV).

Merteuil and Valmont enjoy playing with language as a
particular testimony to their general skills. In the traditional vein
of cuckoldry, the Vicomte has claims on the 'bois' of the
Comtesse de B**'s husband (LIX). Merteuil asks rhetorically of
Valmont: 'le sujet n'en vaut-il pas la peine? en est-il de plus
agréable, dans quelque sens que vous preniez ce mot?' (LXXIV).
In the basic adjectival sense it is 'agréable' to Merteuil, but also
Prévan is an 'agréable' in the modish meaning of a man-about-
town (cf.LXXIX, LXXXI). Merteuil complains that the upper-
class males are all in the country, only the lower orders are in the
capital: 'l'automne ne laisse à Paris presque point d'hommes qui

aient figure humaine' (XXXVIII). (Since it is late August, autumn suggests the traditional time for the harvest, not the romantic season of falling leaves.) She teases Valmont with an ambiguous use of 'bontés': 'vous abusez de mes bontés, même depuis que vous n'en usez plus' (II). Recalling Tourvel's husband and his legal office, Valmont hopes he will lose a case in a manner he does not anticipate (IV).

In fact the novel is full of judicial terms. Belleroche would not approve the 'renouvellement de bail' between Merteuil and Valmont (XX). The three 'inséparables' are judged by some to have submitted even love to 'la loi fondamentale [de] la communauté de biens' (LXXIX). Merteuil states that she will set herself up as a 'juge intègre' evaluating the respective claims of Prévan and Valmont. As far as Valmont is concerned, she already has his 'mémoires' (statements) and his 'affaire est parfaitement instruite' (LXXIV). After talking of her own court case, Merteuil declares Belleroche's has ended, 'hors de cour, dépens compensés' (CXXXIV). In the midst of his crush on the Marquise, Danceny exhibits his new-found wit: 'Comment voulez-vous que je m'intéresse à votre procès, si, perte ou gain, j'en dois également payer les frais par l'ennui de votre absence?' (CXVIII).

For characters who seem to confine their activities to a limited geographical area; namely moving back and forth between Paris and country-houses, Merteuil and Valmont show a surprising fondness for travel imagery. The Marquise upbraids the Vicomte with languishing in Tourvel's company: 'Eh! depuis quand voyagez-vous à petites journées et par des chemins de traverse? Mon ami, quand on veut arriver, des chevaux de poste et la grande route!' (X). How convenient it is to deal with people like Valmont, those '*gens à principes*', whose 'marche réglée' is easily perceived (LXXXV). Valmont is taunted with his lack of invention, for the Marquise deems him unable to 'sortir de la route ordinaire' (CVI). When Valmont has declared his love for Tourvel, he feels he is 'dans la route' and no longer fears that he has been 'égaré' (XXI). He claims that Tourvel has unwittingly taken 'un sentier qui ne permet plus de retour, et dont la pente rapide et dangereuse l'entraîne malgré elle' (XCVI). In the same letter, he explains that he took his time in seducing Cécile for 'une fois sûr d'arriver, pourquoi tant presser le voyage'. As a step in the seduction of Tourvel, Valmont followed 'la grande route des consolations' (CXXV).

Since the army was an appropriate career for an aristocrat, the metaphor of war is an appropriate choice to evoke Valmont's pursuit of women. When he has disposed of the drunken Dutchman, Valmont proclaims himself the 'maître du champ de bataille' (XLVII). To carry out his plans, Valmont explores the layout of a house, and proceeds to 'reconnaître le terrain' (LXXVI). If, together with Merteuil, 'conquérir est [leur] destin', he attacks Tourvel, because her piety and principles make her an 'ennemi digne' (IV). When he recounts her defeat in letter CXXV, he underlines that it was all due to his efforts; it is a 'victoire complète' brought about by a 'campagne pénible', completed by 'de savantes manœuvres'. Merteuil is asked to admire his 'pureté de méthode' in never straying from the 'vrais principes de cette guerre' when he was compelled to 'combattre l'ennemi qui ne voulait que temporiser'. It is he who made 'le choix du terrain et celui des dispositions' and was able to inspire 'la sécurité à l'ennemi, pour le rejoindre plus facilement dans sa retraite'. The detached precision of these military analogies is emblematic of a mind which wishes to leave nothing to chance.

This desire to eliminate chance is also borne out by Valmont's assessments of human comportment. Laclos bestows on his social observers the capacity to sum up human experience. As *moralistes*, Valmont and Merteuil generalize and categorize. Valmont is well aware that a 'femme qui consent à parler d'amour, finit bientôt par en prendre' (LXXVI). He writes disdainfully that people say 'que l'amour rend ingénieux! il abrutit au contraire ceux qu'il domine' (CXXXIII). Laclos accords Valmont insights which recall the analytical powers of Marivaux:

> si les premiers amours paraissent, en général, plus honnêtes, et comme on dit plus purs; s'ils sont au moins plus lents dans leur marche, ce n'est pas, comme on le pense, délicatesse ou timidité, c'est que le cœur, étonné par

un sentiment inconnu, s'arrête pour ainsi dire à chaque
pas, pour jouir du charme qu'il éprouve. (LVII)

These generalizations are typical of a technique found in many
eighteenth-century novels. Individual experience is encapsulated
in pithy remarks which offer a form of knowledge; behaviour is
explicable and assimilable.

Characters in Laclos's novel are not always aware of the full
implications of what they are saying. Cécile is granted the gift of
prophetic accuracy when she tells Danceny: 'nous serons
toujours bien malheureux, et ce ne sera pas ma faute' (XCIV).
Her enthusiasm for Merteuil can be viewed with retrospective
irony when she exclaims 'c'est bien heureux pour moi de l'avoir
connue!' (XXIX). Tourvel claims that Cécile could never be
happier than 'auprès d'une mère aussi digne de toute sa
tendresse et de son respect' (XI). There is unintended irony in
Tourvel's observation to Mme de Volanges: 'M. de Valmont
n'est peut-être qu'un exemple de plus du danger des liaisons'
(XXII). Mme de Volanges is more penetrating than she imagines
in her judgement on Merteuil's character: '[elle] n'a peut-être
d'autre défaut que trop de confiance en ses forces' (XXXII).
Valmont reports the prophetic irony of Tourvel's attempts to
convert him: 'Elle est loin de penser qu'*en plaidant*, pour parler
comme elle, *pour les infortunées que j'ai perdues*, elle parle
d'avance dans sa propre cause' (VI). Even Merteuil is not spared
this ironic twist by Laclos. In letter LIV she says of Danceny:
'l'on peut se brouiller avec celui-là; les raccommodements ne
sont pas dangereux!' How wrong she will be!

Les Liaisons dangereuses is an enactment of the adage that 'all
the world's a stage'. Merteuil and Valmont, as the consummate
artists of *libertinage*, fulfil the roles of both author and actor.
They script scenarios which they perform with panache, indeed
Merteuil claims to 'joindre à l'esprit d'un auteur le talent d'un
comédien' (LXXXI). It is those with limited acting ability, like
Cécile and Tourvel, who are acted upon. High society is a
'théâtre' (LXXXI, XCIX) where brilliant performers yearn to
draw the applause of the gallery. Consequently, the novel
abounds in theatrical devices and terminology.

As is so often the case in comedies (e.g. Beaumarchais's *Le Barbier de Séville*), the master uses a servant to further his amorous designs. Azolan is depicted as a 'trésor d'intrigue, et vrai valet de comédie' who is instructed following theatrical conventions to be 'amoureux de la femme de chambre' (XV). Valmont and Azolan plot to blackmail Tourvel's maid and set up a situation where servant and maid are caught in bed together. Azolan's talent is praised by his master: 'Mon confident, qui joue ses rôles à merveille, donna une petite scène de surprise, de désespoir et d'excuse' (XLIV). Typically, the servant succeeds more rapidly than the master.

Merteuil mocks Danceny concerning Cécile: 'Quand l'héroïne est en scène on ne s'occupe guère de la confidente' (CXLVI). Merteuil requests Valmont to play a 'rôle de confident' to Cécile, for on his success in this function will depend 'le dénouement de cette intrigue' (LXIII). When he writes of Prévan's directorial achievements, Valmont states that 'la scène, restée vide, fut alternativement remplie par les autres acteurs, à peu près de la même manière, et surtout avec le même dénouement' (LXXIX). Merteuil reproaches Valmont with attempting to consign her to the 'troisièmes rôles' (CXXVII). Surrounded by grateful peasants after his spurious act of *bienfaisance*, Valmont compares himself to the 'héros d'un drame, dans la scène du dénouement' (XXI). The comparison suggests the maudlin scenes which were characteristic of the *drame bourgeois* then in fashion.

Merteuil considered making Cécile an 'intrigante subalterne' who could play '*les seconds*' under her (CVI). While in bed with Cécile, Valmont fills the 'entractes' with scandalous tales (CX). The theatrical expression, '*tiers importun*', introduced by Valmont to describe Danceny's presence during his sole meeting with Merteuil, aptly captures the stage-managed situation (CLI, cf.LXXXIII). Valmont likens his existence in his aunt's country-house to the ups and downs of drama: 'n'y ai-je pas jouissances, privations, espoir, incertitude? Qu'a-t-on de plus sur un plus grand théâtre' (XCIX). He enjoys his role in his own drama and takes Merteuil to task for dismissing the delights of his method: 'Eh quoi! ce même spectacle qui vous fait courir au théâtre avec empressement, que vous y applaudissez avec ferveur, le croyez-vous moins attachant dans la réalité?' (XCVI). Elsewhere, in letter LIX, he invites guidance from Merteuil when he asks her to give him 'les réclames de mon rôle' ('réclames' being a technical term indicating what an actor should do next).

Throughout his account of the seduction of Tourvel in letter CXXV, Valmont chooses theatrical language and techniques. At first he surveys what will be 'le théâtre de ma victoire', noting the potential problem presented by a portrait of Tourvel's husband opposite an ottoman. He warms to his task by adopting the 'ton le plus tendre'. Recognizing that he needs to revitalize a 'scène languissante', he flings himself at her feet to facilitate a 'ton dramatique'. A minor setback ensues as he is unable to turn on the tears. All is not lost, however, because women are impressed by a 'grand mouvement' with 'terreur' in support. In melodramatic fashion, he conveys despair by contriving a 'ton bas et sinistre'. He makes progress 'risquant l'enthousiasme'. In another ploy, he decides to 'feindre de [s']éloigner', to pretend to leave the stage. Tourvel cannot bear the thought of such an exit, and through preventing his departure, seals her fate.

Laclos is perhaps also indebted to the theatre in his use of repetition. Merteuil makes her first impact with her mocking command: 'revenez, mon cher Vicomte, revenez' (II). Tourvel is begged by Mme de Volanges to get away from Valmont, 'revenez, revenez, je vous en conjure' (XXXII). Merteuil exhorts Valmont to return to Paris since he is in danger of losing his reputation, 'revenez donc, Vicomte' (CXIII). Valmont imitates her call in letter CXLIV, 'revenez donc au plus tôt'. Even Danceny beseeches Merteuil with 'revenez donc, mon adorable amie' (CXVIII). These ironical echoes parallel the device of comic repetition on the stage. (If Merteuil extols the 'hommages réitérés' of Belleroche in letter X, Valmont vaunts his 'efforts réitérés' in letter XLVIII.)

Labelled as heroes and heroines, characters are ironically presented as anything but exceptional beings. Danceny is portrayed by Valmont as the 'héros de cette aventure' (XLIV) and 'ce beau héros de roman' (LVII), phrases which are repeated in Merteuil's letters (LI, LXIII). Cécile is to be the 'héroïne de ce nouveau roman' (II), and, after her seduction, Valmont reflects on what he should possess to 'perdre l'héroïne' (XCIX). She receives a taunting rebuke from Merteuil in letter CV: 'Rien de mieux, et vous figurez à merveille dans un roman. De la passion, de l'infortune, de la vertu par-dessus tout, que de belles choses'. Prévan is termed the 'héros du jour' by Merteuil when she relates how his stature has been singularly diminished (LXXXV). The slow progress of Danceny irritates the Marquise, who describes him as 'si Céladon', making an adjective out of the name of the hero in D'Urfé's seventeenth-century novel *L'Astrée*. She begs Valmont to push 'ce beau berger à être moins langoureux' (LI).

In passing we may note that novels are mentioned as both a source of distraction and instruction. When the weather prevents him from going hunting, Valmont reads a new novel which he claims would bore even a 'pensionnaire' (LXXIX). Tourvel borrows *Clarissa* from a library (CVII), presumably aware of the tale of the virtuous heroine whose tribulations resemble her own. At a loss in his pursuit of Tourvel, the Vicomte turns in vain to novels for strategies he might employ, without finding any appropriate for the 'caractère de l'héroïne'.[11] He rejects the notion of making her a 'nouvelle Clarisse', and refuses to copy the violence of Richardson's Lovelace (CX). Merteuil likewise turns to literature for inspiration before an assignation with Belleroche: 'je lis un chapitre du *Sopha*, une lettre d'*Héloïse* et deux contes de La Fontaine, pour recorder les différents tons que je voulais prendre' (X) (here 'recorder' means rehearsing the appropriate tone for the appropriate situation). In letter LXXXI, she demonstrates the value of fiction as a guide to society. She speaks of the part played by reading in her programme of self-education: 'J'étudiai nos mœurs dans les romans'. However, Merteuil wishes to make a 'chef-d'œuvre' of her life, outclassing any novelistic invention. She chides Danceny with filling his

[11] Meilcour, a protagonist of Crébillon *fils*, is similarly unsuccessful in seeking inspiration from novels for his next step: 'Je me rappelai alors toutes les occasions que j'avais lues dans les romans de parler à sa maîtresse, et je fus surpris qu'il n'y en eût pas une dont je pusse faire usage', *Les Egarements du cœur et de l'esprit*, p.105.

letters with the hackneyed language found in the 'premier roman du jour' (CXXI). The quality and nature of her original affair with Valmont were exceptional and no-one would believe him if he ever sought to 'perdre' his partner. In her eyes, the truth of their relationship was more incredible than fiction: 'une suite de faits sans vraisemblance, dont le récit sincère aurait l'air d'un roman mal tissu' (LXXXI).

A feature of the novel which I find to be of some importance, and which has sometimes been underestimated, is the incorporation of literary references into the text. Their insertion is an indication of the expectations of a shared culture between correspondents and, by extension, with the reader. (Voltaire, like other contemporaries, was fond of including quotations in his correspondence.) For the average modern reader many of these references will be more or less meaningless without the help of learned annotation. However, for the late eighteenth-century reader who followed the literary scene, they were doubtless *points de repère* which rooted the characters in a cultural experience comparable to his own. As we have seen, Merteuil and Valmont are novel-readers and play-goers who use their storehouse of knowledge to show off to each other. In the second letter of the work there is an allusion to *Clarissa* which would be lost on most readers today. Attempting to whet Valmont's appetite by emphasizing Cécile's adolescent charms, Merteuil refers to her as 'le bouton de rose'. The definite article gives the clue that she is referring to Lovelace's nickname for Rosebud, the young beauty at the White Hart alehouse (*Clarissa*, Vol. I, letter XXIV). Laclos is accordingly borrowing from fiction to authenticate the reading experience of one of his characters; Valmont will doubtless comprehend the allusion. More obvious are the quotations derived from the theatre and novels. They are often to be found in inappropriate places, giving them a parodic ring, and are drawn from a wide variety of authors, e.g. Racine (LXXI), Voltaire (LXXXV, XCIX), Rousseau (CX). Merteuil's and Valmont's purpose in employing these quotations, which are not all totally accurate, in contexts out of keeping with their original source, is probably further evidence of their scorn for accepted and respected values.

Authors' works, like all else in their world, are merely a means to an end and may be used and abused at will.

Laclos turns to the Bible as another source of references. Tourvel sees herself as aiding the prodigal son to return to respectability (CXXIV). It is Merteuil, however, who makes the greater use of scriptural allusions. She pictures herself as a new Delilah besting modern Samsons (LXXXI). She writes of consoling Cécile: 'Dieu! qu'elle était belle! Ah! si Magdeleine était ainsi, elle dut être bien plus dangereuse pénitenté que pécheresse' (LXIII, cf.Luke 7.38). She compares Tourvel to the poor man picking up the crumbs from the rich man's table (CXIII, cf.Luke 16.21). She takes delight in the situation which leads both mother and daughter to seek her advice: 'N'est-il pas plaisant, en effet, de consoler pour et contre, et d'être le seul agent de deux intérêts directement contraires' (LXIII). She adopts the role of 'ange consolateur', and goes to 'visiter mes amis dans leur affliction' in parodic imitation of James 1.27. On one occasion, angered by Valmont, she tells him scathingly that he is 'riche en bonne opinion de [lui]-même' (CXXVII, cf.Proverbs 26.5).

Religious terminology is also subjected to perverse manipulation. Valmont informs Merteuil: 'nous prêchons la foi chacun de notre côté, il me semble que dans cette mission d'amour, vous avez fait plus de prosélytes que moi' (IV). In the same letter, the Vicomte imagines himself becoming a 'saint de village', a status Tourvel appears to confer on him when recounting his charity to the peasants (XXIII).

As is the case in so many eighteenth-century novels, we are frequently made aware of editorial intrusion and organization through the use of footnotes. A note accompanying the *Préface du Rédacteur* informs the reader in the customary manner that the names of the correspondents have been altered, a tactic of discretion asserting bogus *vraisemblance*. People (I, XIII, LXXXV) and places (CI, CVII) are identified, past relationships summarized (II), fashionable terms explained (II, LXXXV). Readers are referred to other letters for clarification of points or events (XLI, LXXXV, CXIII), some letters are reported lost (XVI, LI, LXXVI, CXII), others have been suppressed to avoid tedious repetitions (VII, XXXIX, LXXV), still others offer scholarly notes regarding the sources of literary quotations (LVIII, LXVI, LXXI, CXXXIII). We are told how the collection came to be put together (CLXIX), and supplied with a tantalizing glimpse of what happened next to Merteuil and Cécile (CLXXV). Elsewhere, we are offered explicit judgments on the actions and motives of the characters: Tourvel is somewhat dishonest (XXII), Danceny a fibber (LXV), Merteuil is contemptuous of religion (LI), and only those who have been truly in love could appreciate Danceny's heartfelt 'je vous aime' (XLVI). All such interventions remind the reader that he has in his hands a carefully structured work in which Laclos has endeavoured to make every detail relevant.

Throughout this chapter the emphasis has been on the use and abuse of language. It should not close, however, without some reference to non-verbal communication. In certain circumstances, glances and gestures may be more effective than words. Danceny tells Cécile, 'qu'ai-je à vous dire, que mes regards, mon embarras, ma conduite et même mon silence ne vous aient dit avant moi?' (XVII).

Valmont notes the effect he has on Tourvel through her blushing, her heart beating faster, her glances, her gripping his hand (VI, XXIII, XCIX). He uses his eyes to convey his interest in Tourvel, and she cannot but respond: 'Alors s'établit entre nous cette convention tacite, premier traité de l'amour timide, qui, pour satisfaire le besoin mutuel de se voir, permet aux regards de se succéder en attendant qu'ils se confondent'. He recognizes that she is experiencing a new emotion and, after ensuring that the others members of the 'cercle' are deep in conversation, he continues: 'Je tâchai d'obtenir de ses yeux qu'ils parlassent franchement leur langage [...] Peu à peu nos yeux, accoutumés à se rencontrer, se fixèrent plus longtemps; enfin ils ne se quittèrent plus, et j'aperçus dans les siens cette douce langueur, signal heureux de l'amour et du désir' (LXXVI). Whatever her words might deny, Valmont can detect the truth in her eyes. Merteuil similarly excels at sending contrived signals, as we see in her burgeoning relationship with Prévan: 'nos yeux parlèrent beaucoup. Je dis nos yeux: je devrais dire les siens; car les miens n'eurent qu'un langage, celui de la surprise. Il dut penser que je m'étonnais et m'occupais excessivement de l'effet prodigieux qu'il faisait sur moi' (LXXXV). Merteuil's feigned response deceives Prévan into misinterpreting the signals and contributing to his downfall. Non-verbal communication may thus be regarded as playing a significant part in the development of the novel on both a voluntary and involuntary basis.[12]

[12] In chapter twelve of *Des femmes et de leur éducation* Laclos declares: 'On sait assez que les grands mouvements de l'âme ou des sens se peignent dans les yeux en surmontant même les obstacles qu'on leur oppose. Tel est le droit de la nature; l'art a cherché à l'imiter, et y est parvenu: l'usage en est fréquent au théâtre, l'abus s'en est glissé dans la société et les regards sont devenus menteurs et perfides' (*1*, p.434).

5. Import and Impact

Any account of the import and impact of the work must assess the significance of both the *Préface du Rédacteur* and the *Avertissement de l'Editeur*. The preface contains the usual eighteenth-century claims concerning the authenticity of the letters in the 'recueil', and the explanation of the editor's role in including only the letters which are necessary 'soit à l'intelligence des événements, soit au développement des caractères'. The editor is of course the author in disguise. In classical fashion the author/editor asserts that the work's function is its 'utilité' and its 'agrément', in other words, *plaire et instruire*. It is to serve the cautionary purpose of pointing out twin truths of contemporary application that : 'toute femme qui consent à recevoir dans sa société un homme sans mœurs, finit par en devenir la victime' and that 'toute mère est au moins imprudente, qui souffre qu'un autre qu'elle ait la confiance de sa fille'. Here is the well-rehearsed justification of the novel highlighting the pitfalls of society, as Georges May has shown (*17*, pp.131-35).

However, the statements of the preface, which insist on the relevance of the work to the society of the day, are contradicted by the *Avertissement*. There we are advised that we are almost certainly being offered only a 'roman'. The author himself has destroyed the necessary *vraisemblance* by situating the events in an age which has become so enlightened that the iniquitous behaviour of some characters beggars belief. Moreover, nowadays rich young heiresses do not lock themselves away in convents, nor would an attractive young 'Présidente' die from grief. Laclos is here playing a sophisticated game of bluff and counter-bluff. At least the habitual novel-reader would, by this late date in the century, be resistant to swallowing whole the conventional assertion of authenticity, and Laclos accordingly treats him with some subtlety. His warning does not solely call into question the genuine origins of the text, but also issues an ironic appeal to a social reality accessible to the reader. In the latter context, the reader might well feel that the publisher is wrong, and that the characters in the text are perhaps accurate. One could propose a certain analogy with Valmont's tactic of proffering half-truths the better to ensnare.

But are we to take *Les Liaisons dangereuses* as a representative portrayal of aristocratic society on the verge of dissolution? The coming of the French Revolution in 1789, just seven years after the appearance of Laclos's novel, has prompted some to arrive at such an interpretation. (A comparison could be made with Jean Renoir's film of 1939, *La Règle du jeu*, where a country-house party could be judged to symbolize the decadence of the ruling classes immediately prior to World War II.) We are certainly presented with a society pervaded by a constant dread of boredom. Merteuil and Valmont, if they are not actively engaged in some piece of skulduggery, spend their time in planning, and savouring in advance, their future exploits. Cécile has not been educated for any worthwhile activity. Tourvel indulges in charitable works to relieve the tedium of her existence, and one wonders whether life was any richer with her husband around. Mme de Volanges takes a superficial interest in her daughter's forthcoming nuptials, but is basically a gossip on the look-out for verbal ammunition. Danceny moons around and is hardly preparing for his career in the Order of Malta. Mme de Rosemonde seems to be confined to her country-house. She is grateful to have her nephew's lively company and to learn of events in the *monde*. In general, the social round is punctuated by meals, card-games and the type of theatre-going so much condemned by Rousseau. True, minor characters such as Prévan and Gercourt are in the army, yet even that profession appears to be more connected with their social rank than their patriotic utility. Tourvel's husband is the sole noble character in the work who seems to be busy, but then he is in Dijon and none of his letters is deemed worthy of inclusion. One may note that during his imprisonment Laclos informed his wife that he found 'occupation' far preferable to 'amusement' (*I*, p.830). Whether he entertained the same thought a decade or so before when he was composing his novel can only be a matter of speculation.

Nevertheless, one is justified in asserting that this aristocratic world is unattractive, with its behaviour regulated by an etiquette based on social standing. The refined language, demanded by *honnêteté*, has become a camouflage for anti-social conduct. Language has become a 'liaison dangereuse'. A notorious rake like Valmont is admitted everywhere, since he has rank and social graces; it is appearances that count. Here Laclos is echoing Rousseau's attacks on the superficiality of the *monde*.

However, to regard Tourvel, as some have done, as a representative of the bourgeoisie seduced by a debauched aristocrat is historical nonsense. She probably belongs to the socially integrated *noblesse de robe*, which had a reputation for Jansenist leanings, so that Laclos could add plausibility to her austere principles. In fact, it is difficult to envisage how one could introduce the notion of class criticism here, for even if she had been of an inferior social status, her seduction would have been in no way related to this inferiority. There is no hint of a more up-market version of the wicked squire ruining the village maiden, indeed Valmont would be interested only in getting the better of a social equal.

If Laclos had wished to stress the political dimensions, he could have developed his picture of peasants in straitened circumstances. We are told that Valmont's servant had no difficulty finding poverty in the countryside. In disbursing fifty-six *livres*, the Vicomte saved five people from being reduced 'à la paille et au désespoir' (XXI). Laclos could have made more of Merteuil's observation: 'Nous ne sommes plus au temps de Madame de Sévigné. Le luxe absorbe tout: on le blâme, mais il faut l'imiter; et le superflu finit par priver du nécessaire' (CIV). This comment on economic matters shows an awareness of historical change and has the ring of what was conventional wisdom for some at the time. The novelist could have further exploited the judicial corruption hinted at in letter CXXXIV. The fact is that Laclos did not choose to provide more extensive coverage of these aspects of the society of his day.

On another oft-debated issue I would like to suggest that there is nothing in the events of the novel which links it exclusively to the final decades of the century; the portrayal of seduction in high society was hardly a literary innovation. What does tie it down to the late eighteenth century are a few historical landmarks. The 'petite poste', mail delivered by postmen in Paris, which is referred to in letter LXIII, was instituted in 1760. Gercourt was probably stationed in Corsica because the island had been ceded by Genoa to France in 1768. Some of the literary allusions clearly situate the novel in the second half of the century e.g. *La Nouvelle Héloïse* (1761), *Le Siège de Calais* (1765).

Yet, although one is hesitant to state that a particular historical moment produced *Les Liaisons dangereuses*, it is none the less a work which is redolent of its times. A glance at the place of religion in the novel may be of value here. Given her charitable activities and her 'hopes' for Valmont's conversion, Tourvel's attachment to religion can be considered as genuine. Even if she has not undergone some profound religious experience, there can be no doubt that her adultery costs her far more than Flaubert's Emma Bovary. However, when she is finally disabused, she is devastated by a feeling of betrayal rather than of sin. The administration of the last sacraments notwithstanding, one senses her earthly salvation was of more moment for her.

Merteuil and Valmont have no religious 'prejudices', and the latter has no qualms about playing the *faux dévot* after playing the *faux sensible* in the scene with the peasants. His death appears as a social exit and not as an entrance to eternal damnation — metaphysical considerations do not touch this Don Juan. Indeed, religion is presented as an activity to which conformist members of society like Mme de Volanges pay lip-service. Towards the end of the work Mme de Rosemonde proposes conservative guidelines: 'si on était éclairé sur son véritable bonheur, on ne le chercherait jamais hors des bornes prescrites par les lois et la religion' (CLXXI). Is it significant that man-made laws precede religion? In any case, religion appears to fulfil a utilitarian function as a social restraint in a manner recalling the ideas of Voltaire.

If metaphysical dimensions and sanctions are absent, moral and social problems are not. Pre-eminent amongst the latter is assuredly the problem of evil. If, in terms of conventional morality, Merteuil's and Valmont's actions may be deemed individually and socially harmful, are we to attribute their behaviour to inherent aspects of human nature or to the world in which they live? Is their unscrupulous conduct to be ascribed to evil as a perennial component of the human condition or to the historical situation in which they find themselves? In other words, is evil ontological or sociological? In my opinion it would be reckless to propose a clear-cut answer. Certainly in chapter II of *Des femmes et de leur éducation* Laclos, following Rousseau, suggests it is sociological:

> Les hommes ont voulu tout perfectionner et ils ont tout corrompu; ils se sont chargés de chaînes, puis ils se sont plaints d'être accablés sous leur poids; insensés et injustes, ils ont abandonné la nature qui les rendait heureux, puis ils l'ont calomniée, en l'accusant des maux que cet abandon leur causait. (*1*, p.393)

Man has gone astray, and Laclos quotes Seneca in support: 'Le mal est sans remède quand les vices se sont changés en mœurs' (*1*, p.389).

Is this the case in *Les Liaisons dangereuses*? As we have seen, members of the leisured classes have both the opportunity and the potential to sate their desires; predators and victims alike seek distractions from *ennui*. It is then possible to suggest that in a differently organized society, with more time-consuming activities, such happenings might be impossible. However, can we charge society with the responsibility for the whole range of Merteuil's and Valmont's actions? Are their respective wishes to 'perdre' Prévan and Cécile to be imputed to the shape of society? It can be argued so, though some may find aspects of their cruelty rather gratuitous. Mme de Volanges, who is not evil but frequently inept, tells Tourvel: 'L'humanité n'est parfaite dans aucun genre, pas plus dans le mal que dans le bien. Le scélérat a ses vertus, comme l'honnête homme a ses faiblesses'

(XXXII). Could she be speaking for Laclos in this generalization? The only honest answer is that one cannot say, though most of us would probably agree with her, and her statement does apply in varying doses to the characters in the work. Laclos's views on evil may not be clear from what Baudelaire called a 'livre de sociabilité' (*6*, p.70), but it is surely safe to infer that society could be improved, if not perfected, that *liaisons heureuses* are possible. Laclos's choice of title stresses social connections rather than giving star-billing to individuals. Mme de Volanges points out that Valmont's behaviour causes distress in that most basic of social units, the family. Evil is a crime against sociability.

Following literary tradition, Laclos punishes vice. He does not, however, reward virtue, nor does he have his *libertins* rehabilitated by true love at the end. Again Mme de Volanges provides a balanced summary: 'Je vois bien dans tout cela les méchants punis; mais je n'y trouve nulle consolation pour les malheureuses victimes' (CLXXIII). Retribution is meted out to Valmont from the avenging sword of Danceny and the former thereby receives appropriate, if illegal, punishment. Merteuil is also subjected to social punishment when she is cold-shouldered in the theatre after her letters are released, and further chastized by losing her lawsuit. She had earlier been confident of winning her case, and one wonders whether she lost through her waning prestige and influence, rather than by due legal process. But catching smallpox is of a different order. Unquestionably the disease was widespread in the eighteenth century; Voltaire caught it and Louis XV died from it.[13] A present-day novelist would perhaps choose cancer as an equivalent device. Nevertheless, the actions and reactions in the novel up until this point have been humanly or socially motivated, and the disease will strike many to be an unwarranted and unnecessary 'supernatural' intrusion. Laclos can be accused of being heavy-handed here, and one can only assume that he wanted to make her condemnation unequivocally clear, a deduction confirmed

[13] Robert Favre asserts that 'la grande cause de mort est, sans contredit, presque tout au long du XVIIIe siècle, la petite vérole', *La Mort dans la littérature et la pensée françaises au siècle des lumières* (Presses Universitaires de Lyon, 1978), p.46. Julie contracts smallpox in Rousseau's *La Nouvelle Héloïse*.

by the final footnote in the work.

If Laclos set out to depict the ravages of vice, during the composition of the novel he may well have found Merteuil and Valmont were assuming attractions that he had not anticipated. Just as Flaubert would seem to have felt a sneaking admiration for his well-intentioned oafs, Bouvard and Pécuchet, so Laclos may have acquired an ambiguous admiration for his pair of miscreants. There is a danger of making villains one-dimensional creatures, which Laclos happily avoided, but at the cost of making his vicious characters attractive and consequently 'realistic'. Diderot's Neveu de Rameau remarks that 's'il importe d'être sublime en quelque genre, c'est surtout en mal' (*3*, p.486). Merteuil as well as Valmont are 'sublimes' as they captivate the reader and would qualify for Diderot's epithet of 'originaux'. Indeed, so concerned was the successful novelist, Mme Riccoboni, that she wrote: 'j'invite M. de Laclos à ne jamais orner le vice des agréments qu'il a prêtés à Mme de Merteuil' (*1*, p.757). In reply, Laclos stated he believed that 'en peignant le vice, il pouvait lui laisser tous les agréments dont il n'est que trop souvent orné; et il a voulu que cette parure dangereuse et séduisante ne pût affaiblir un moment l'impression d'horreur que le vice doit toujours exciter' (*1*, p.758). Whether at the outset he was striving for such an effect one cannot say, but he was patently aware of what he had achieved. He declared in the same letter, however, that Tourvel and Rosemonde should prove an effective counterbalance. All in all, one senses the artist was greater than the *moraliste*, and one recalls Gide's dictum: 'c'est avec les beaux sentiments qu'on fait de la mauvaise littérature'.[14]

Certainly all the characters are affected adversely by the events of the novel. We are shown a society whose members willy-nilly destroy themselves, destroy others or reveal themselves impotent to grasp the significance of what is happening around them. Valmont and Merteuil fail to live up to their much vaunted ideal of self-interest and detachment. Valmont hypocritically denies his attachment to Tourvel, however acutely and repeatedly Merteuil points out his

---

[14]André Gide, *Journal 1939-1942* (Paris, Gallimard, 1949) p.82.

weakness. Merteuil is pricked by jealousy when she realizes the strength of Tourvel's hold over Valmont. Her revenge when she goads him into despatching her 'letter' to the Présidente is not just an act of the intellect. Despite Tourvel's turmoil, her flight like a hunted animal, indeed despite her better judgement, the Présidente's final surrender is an abdication of reason and a submission to overwhelming passion. None of these three characters is capable of a successful juggling act with the varied desires and restraints coexisting in the human personality. The trio are all extremists in their respective ways and delude themselves they can rise above common humanity in their absolutist paths, eliminate chance, and pre-ordain the future. They blind themselves to the limitations of nature and culture. Merteuil and Valmont fail to live up to their principles, and it is this inconsistency, not their immorality, which brings about their downfall, namely their failures as libertines and not their libertine philosophy. They both try to foist a single ideal on a multi-faceted reality; for such intelligent characters, this is a quite quixotic delusion. The heroes of intelligence end up as its victims. Their illusions are different in degree, but not in kind, from Emma Bovary's or Jean-Baptiste Clamence's in Camus's *La Chute*. One of the novel's great merits is the puncturing of reductionist idealism, the futile attempt to impose an order on the dynamism of life — in a very different way Diderot was illustrating the same point in *Jacques le fataliste*.

What is Laclos's conception of the role of the artist? A statement emanating from his correspondence with Mme Riccoboni is worth reflection: 'il me semble que le droit du moraliste, soit dramatique soit romancier, ne commence qu'où les lois se taisent' (*1*, p.767). The actions of some of the characters in *Les Liaisons dangereuses* may not infringe the criminal law, but they unquestionably assault the dignity of the individual. Taken at face value, Laclos's claim bestows on literature the lofty status of moral commentary, and is in line with the didactic function of reading which he will later define as 'une seconde éducation qui supplée à l'insuffisance de la première'. The vicarious experience offered by reading is useful since 'l'expérience personnelle est souvent chère et toujours tardive' (*1*, p.434). If this is so, in pointing out the potential 'liaisons dangereuses' in society, Laclos may indeed be following in the footsteps of the Molière of *Tartuffe*. But he is also, I suggest, following the eighteenth-century *philosophes* in their mission to spread enlightenment. To take an example from the novel, Laclos is offering a clear criticism of convent education. Such a secluded upbringing in no way prepares a young girl for the pressures and problems of a sudden insertion into society. Valmont observes that her education will not have informed Cécile 'à combien de périls divers est exposée la timide innocence' (XCVI). The disabused Danceny mounts an attack on the inadequacies of a convent upbringing. How could any young girl, leaving a convent 'sans expérience et presque sans idées', with 'une égale ignorance du bien et du mal', be expected to resist the dangers of the 'monde' (CLXXIV)? This letter, the penultimate in the work, is strategically placed where a *leçon* may be drawn. It is only too understandable that Cécile and Tourvel prove easy prey.

Whatever Laclos's intentions were as a writer, his readers have reacted differently over the years. In his own day we have seen how anxious Mme Riccoboni was about his alluring portrayal of vice, and his authorship of the work was held against him by his enemies during the Revolution. It would be fascinating to possess a wide sample of the reactions of contemporary readers, other than those of writers and professional critics. Doubtless some readers would have read it as a *roman-à-clef*, and speculated on the originals of the main characters, always a titillating temptation. Others may have wondered how much of the author is transferred to Valmont? Still others might have obtained a voyeuristic *frisson* from this encounter with an aristocratic world, paraded their *sensibilité* with mandatory tears at Tourvel's fate while contemplating with true or feigned horror the machinations of Merteuil and Valmont. But, most importantly of all for Laclos's avowed purpose, would the novel have been for them merely one of those 'most delightful substitutes for bodily dissipation',[15] or

---

[15] This definition of novels occurs in Mary Wollstonecraft's *Mary and the Wrongs of Woman* (Oxford U.P., 1983) p.2.

would they actually have learnt something from reading the novel? Would they have been sensitized to the dangers of high-society living? Would the work have been a useful guide-book for the newcomer to the *monde*? One remembers that in *L'Ingénu* (Ch.XII), Voltaire's Huron was delighted by Molière who introduced him to 'les mœurs de Paris et du genre humain'.[16]

Yet what if someone did not read with improvement in mind? There is the case of the Neveu de Rameau who turns to literature with interest, and appropriately comments on Molière:

> Quand je lis *le Tartuffe*, je me dis: Sois hypocrite si tu veux, mais ne parle pas comme l'hypocrite. Garde des vices qui te sont utiles; mais n'en aie ni le ton, ni les apparences qui te rendraient ridicule. Pour se garantir de ce ton, de ces apparences, il faut les connaître; or, ces auteurs en ont fait des peintures excellentes. (*3*, p.476)

The Neveu reads authors such as Molière and La Bruyère the better to dissimulate — would Merteuil do otherwise? In common with so many other writers of his day, Laclos seems unable to digest the evidence of his own works; if fictional readers abuse knowledge from literature, why can't real ones?

Modern readers no doubt vary in their responses. In spite of sympathy for Tourvel, most are more impressed by Merteuil and Valmont. (For similar reasons, the witty Mary Crawford is more engaging than the worthy Fanny Price in Jane Austen's *Mansfield Park*.) We like villains when they are securely contained in the pages of a book or the images of a television soap-opera. Compared to the eighteenth-century reader, we have possibly fewer problems distinguishing between literal and imaginative belief, though that is a moot point. We may find it easier to sympathize with the impossible love of that disreputable double act, des Grieux and Manon Lescaut, or admire the sincerity of the murdering Meursault in Camus's

[16] Paul, Bernardin de Saint-Pierre's hero, is likewise struck by 'la lecture de nos romans à la mode, pleins de mœurs et de maximes licencieuses; et quand il sut que ces romans renfermaient une peinture véritable des sociétés de l'Europe, il craignait, non sans quelque apparence de raison, que Virginie ne vînt à s'y corrompre et à l'oublier', *Paul et Virginie*, édition établie et présentée par Jean Ehrard (Paris, Gallimard, Collection Folio, 1984) p.184.

L'Etranger. They are all fictional creatures who can never be our next-door neighbours. In making *Les Liaisons dangereuses* an unquestioned classic, the permissive age has made respectable the least permissive of books.

Careful reading, especially re-reading, of the text reveals a master craftsman at work. Laclos developed an overall conception of where his novel was going, unlike some of his contemporaries who published their fiction in instalments and without necessarily having a clear idea where their narratives would end. He was able to organize a complex series of interrelationships into an organic whole. It is only through minute analysis that one recognizes the care that Laclos brought to its final version; the astute placing of letters; the parallel destinies of Cécile and Tourvel who reply unwisely to letters and unthinkingly embark on 'liaisons dangereuses'; the ironies which become apparent only when one has read the full text. One realizes that its epistolary form is essential to its success, hence the failures of the film adaptations. Even the ingenious use of telephones or tape-recorders would not produce comparable results. Replying to letters proves Tourvel's interest in Valmont. Letters show up Cécile's shortcomings and embarrassment, they highlight Merteuil's and Valmont's verbal skills. Indeed, Merteuil and Valmont probably derive more pleasure from writing about their evil deeds than perpetrating them. Despite Merteuil's denial of the power of letters (XXXIII), Valmont basically seduces Tourvel through the written word in a manner impossible in conversation. However clear-sighted as individuals they may be, all the correspondents possess only a limited grasp of what is going on. There being no omniscient character or author with whom the reader may identify, the letter-novel is one of the most 'realistic' and 'natural' modes of fiction.[17] It was a most appropriate form in such a great age of correspondents, though even today we still

[17] In my view it is wrong to credit any one character with a pre-eminent role in the work. I would disagree with Dorothy Thelander (*27*, p.81) that Valmont is the 'pivotal character' and with Shirley Jones that Merteuil seems 'to dominate the novel' ('Literary and philosophical elements in *Les Liaisons dangereuses*: the case of Merteuil', *French Studies*, XXXVIII (1984), p.168).

write and receive letters. The vogue of epistolary fiction ended in the eighteenth century although there have been letter-novels since; the well-known American novelist John Barth published one entitled *Letters* in 1979.[18]

To my mind Laclos was the most successful practitioner of the form, Richardson getting too bogged down in minutiae in *Clarissa* and Rousseau too prone to digressions in *La Nouvelle Héloïse*. Laclos strove to eliminate unnecessary items from his novel, to make everything strictly relevant. He was to criticize Fanny Burney for being carried away 'trop facilement par des détails, par des scènes entières qui ne servent ni à l'intérêt de l'action, ni au développement des caractères' (*1*, p.469). His artistry can be summed up by quoting Valmont out of context: 'Ce sont ces petits détails qui donnent la vraisemblance, et la vraisemblance rend les mensonges sans conséquence, en ôtant le désir de les vérifier' (LXXXIV). Laclos's planning and attention to detail carry the reader along, and for a few hours create 'un petit monde qui absorbe toute notre attention et nos affections' (*1*, p.511).

In the closing years of the Ancien Régime, when so many works were awash with sentimentality, Laclos was, as Jean Fabre observes (*14*, pp.147-48), one of the few writers still to make a pervasive use of irony. In the course of this study I have often applied the adjective 'ironical' to a variety of remarks and situations. In truth the work is dominated by irony. How ironical it is that Tourvel should discover love and happiness as a result of Valmont's lies; that for Valmont acting a part with Tourvel becomes a vehicle for self-discovery rather that an illustration of self-mastery. The premeditated victory of the seducer over the victim becomes in some measure the unpremeditated defeat of the seducer by the victim. How ironical it is that Merteuil and Valmont should destroy each other — 'ce sont les bons nageurs qui se noient' (LXXVI) — and end up as further exemplars of the commonplace theme of the

---

[18] Margaret Mauldon has examined Stendhal's use of letters in 'Generic survival: *Le Rouge et le Noir* and the epistolary tradition', *French Studies*, XXXVIII (1984), 414-22. Bernard Bray has commented on contemporary versions of the format in 'Transformations du roman épistolaire au XXe siècle en France', *Romanistische Zeitschrift für Literaturgeschichte*, I (1977), 23-39.

trompeur trompé. Despite the horrendous circumstances at the end of the novel, in classical fashion, the two lovers are reunited in the grave. Using irony Laclos shapes the reader's response and strips away the masks of deception and self-delusion of the characters. He does not descend to moralizing and preachifying to get a message across; his appeal is primarily to the intellect and not to the emotions. His is an art of analysis, rather than suggestion; for him, man is, or at least may be, intelligible.

If, as I would contend, he is offering us amidst other things a cautionary tale, as Voltaire does in his *contes*, he is seeking ultimately a detached appreciation. People of all ages like stories, and Laclos gave us a fine one. In his review of the *Voyage de La Pérouse* in 1797 he pointed out how successive generations world-wide have wished to leave a monument to their earthly sojourn, and how 'écriture' possesses 'le magique pouvoir [qui] exprime et fixe à la fois le sentiment et la pensée' (*1*, p.470). In *Les Liaisons dangereuses* Laclos mixed the necessary ingredients to produce a dish which *fins becs* will continue to relish in both its content and presentation.

Afterword

This study was completed in early 1985 and in the intervening years scholarly interest in *Les Liaisons dangereuses* has continued unabated. The *Bibliographical Supplement* provides only a selection of relevant studies. Arguably the most weighty contribution is the biography by Georges Poisson (*52*). While it contains no major revelations, it supplies fresh details and has replaced a dated biography (*10*) as the standard source of reference. A number of studies have dealt with the role of readers, both real and fictional (*37, 54, 55, 57*). The morality or otherwise of the tale still attracts critical attention (*33, 50*). The differing quality of the relationships, on the grounds of gender, between the male and female characters has been soundly distinguished (*38*). Much illuminating work on one of the novelist's important precursors, Crébillon, has appeared in recent years and their names have been linked in a monograph (*35*). Some pioneering research on the eighteenth-century reaction to the novel in the English-speaking world has appeared (*40*). The Irish political activist, William Drennan, had read the English version by 1786 and pronounced it 'a most masterly piece of dangerous seduction in style and sentiment' (*41*).

However, the fame of the text has been considerably widened by the stage and film versions. It is perhaps one of the ironies of literary history that an epistolary novel so clearly rooted in the social and literary practice of its own day should appeal to a modern audience through its depiction of sexual politics. Furthermore, it is perhaps surprising that a text justly celebrated for the power of words should prove a success in a visual medium. Nevertheless, as was the case in the eighteenth century with the translation from one language to another, the translation to the stage and screen has necessitated substantial changes. Christopher Hampton's theatrical adaptation was acclaimed immediately in 1985 and justifiably so. Yet, as Bill

Overton has observed, Hampton 'greatly reduces the ambiguity' of the text and has produced 'a play too neat and smooth, too consumable, to carry the disturbing questions of Laclos's novel' (*51*, pp.264, 273). The film versions likewise tend to be marked with modernising resonances, *Dangerous Liaisons* (Stephen Frears, 1988) and *Valmont* (Miloš Forman, 1989). (One recalls also *Les Liaisons dangereuses 1960* by Roger Vadim in 1959.) The Frears and Forman adaptations have been subjected to a comparative study by Robin Lefère who differentiates their approaches in an incisive manner. (*47*). Lefère notes a crucial distinction between the novel and any modern version, 'le langage, était beaucoup plus qu'aujourd'hui, instrument de domination' (p.141). While bemoaning some of the distortions wreaked by the screen adaptations, Laurent Versini effectively highlights the outstanding attributes of the original novel (*58*). Most critics prefer the Frears version. Ultimately, the stage and film adaptations can be judged only as successful creations on their own terms, as competent examples of work in their chosen medium. For those familiar with the novel, nothing could replace the intricacies of the battle of words since their imaginative and evocative power is in fact diminished rather than enhanced by any visual supplement.

Select Bibliography

PRIMARY TEXTS

Les Liaisons dangereuses has appeared in a variety of cheap and de luxe editions in recent years as David Coward records (see *9*, pp.292-93). The paperback editions published by Garnier-Flammarion (1996; see *2* below) and Gallimard, Collection Folio (1972) are perfectly adequate for students and the general reader.

1. Choderlos de Laclos, *Œuvres complètes*, ed. Laurent Versini (Paris, Gallimard, Bibliothèque de la Pléiade, 1979).
2. *Les Liaisons dangereuses*, ed. René Pomeau (Paris, Lettres françaises, Collection de l'Imprimerie Nationale, 1981), 2 vols. Pomeau's edition, containing a substantial introduction and helpful annotation, was reprinted in the GF series in 1996 with an updated bibliography.
3. Diderot, *Œuvres romanesques*, ed. H. Bénac, revue pour l'établissement du texte, l'introduction et les notes par L. Pérol (Paris, Garnier, 1981).
4. Richardson, *Clarissa or, the History of a Young Lady* (London, Dent, 1932), 4 vols.

CRITICAL STUDIES

There follows a short selection of studies which provide useful guidance. Fuller bibliographies may be consulted in David Coward (*9*) and Colette Michael (*18*).

5. Barny, R., 'Madame de Merteuil et la critique du libertinage', *Dix-huitième Siècle*, XV (1983), 369-88. A heretical article disputing the generally accepted interpretations of Merteuil's motivation.
6. Baudelaire, C., 'Notes sur *Les Liaisons dangereuses*', *Œuvres complètes*, ed. Claude Pichois (Paris, Gallimard, Bibliothèque de la Pléiade, 1976), vol. 2, pp.66-75.

7. Belaval, Y., *Choderlos de Laclos* (Paris, Seghers, 1972). A concise introduction to Laclos and his novel which offers extracts from his works.

8. Coulet, H., 'Le style imitatif dans le roman épistolaire français des siècles classiques', *Revue d'Histoire Littéraire de la France*, LXXXV (1985), 3-17. Judicious observations on stylistic practice in the French letter-novel.

9. Coward, D., 'Laclos studies, 1968-1982', *Studies on Voltaire and the Eighteenth Century*, CCXIX (Oxford, Voltaire Foundation, 1983), 289-330. An excellent survey of modern criticism on Laclos.

10. Dard, E., *Le Général Choderlos de Laclos, auteur des 'Liaisons dangereuses', 1741-1803* (Paris, Perrin, 1905; reprinted in 1920 and 1936). An ageing but still valuable biography.

11. Delmas, A. and Y., *A la recherche des 'Liaisons dangereuses'* (Paris, Mercure de France, 1964). Examines the critical fortunes of the novel.

12. Delon, M., 'Valeurs sensibles, valeurs libertines de l'énergie', *Romantisme*, XLVI (1984), 3-13. A penetrating analysis of the idea of 'énergie' in late eighteenth-century novels.

13. Duranton, H., *'Les Liaisons dangereuses ou le miroir ennemi'*, *Revue des Sciences Humaines*, XXXIX (1974), 125-43. An assessment which challenges traditional interpretations.

14. Fabre, J., *'Les Liaisons dangereuses*, roman de l'ironie', in his *Idées sur le roman de madame de Lafayette au marquis de Sade* (Paris, Klincksieck, 1979), pp.143-65 (first published in *Missions et démarches de la critique: mélanges offerts au professeur J.A. Vier* (Paris, Klincksieck, 1973), pp.651-72. Analyses Laclos's intentions and relates the novel to its literary-historical context.

15. Free, L.R. (ed.), *Critical Approaches to the 'Liaisons dangereuses'* (Madrid, José Porrúa Turanzas, 1978). A collection of traditional and 'structuralist' readings of uneven quality.

16. *Laclos et le libertinage: actes du colloque du bicentenaire des 'Liaisons dangereuses'* (Paris, Presses Universitaires de France, 1983). Papers devoted to Laclos's novel and its influence as well as previous treatments of *libertinage*.

17. May, G., *Le Dilemme du roman au XVIIIe siècle (1715-1761)* (Paris, Presses Universitaires de France, 1963). Essential background reading for the development of the novel in eighteenth-century France

18. Michael, C.V., *Choderlos de Laclos: the man, his works, his critics. An annotated bibliography* (New York and London, Garland Publishing, 1982). A descriptive rather than a critical bibliography.

19. Mylne, V., *The Eighteenth-Century French Novel : techniques of illusion* (revised edition, Cambridge University Press, 1981: first edition, Manchester University Press, 1965). A classic study of fictional technique in eighteenth-century France.

20. Pappas, J., 'Le moralisme des *Liaisons dangereuses*', *Dix-huitième Siècle* II (1970), 265-96. A lively, controversial article which accords an important role to Mme de Rosemonde.

21. Pomeau, R., *Laclos* (Paris, Hatier, 1975). A short balanced survey of Laclos and his work.

22. *Revue d'Histoire Littéraire de la France*, LXXXII (1982). A collection of stimulating articles on *Les Liaisons dangereuses* produced as a bicentenary commemoration of the novel's publication.

23. Rosbottom, R. C., *Choderlos de Laclos* (Boston, Twayne Publishers, 1978). A demanding study but one of the best in the Twayne series.

24. Rousset, J., 'Une forme littéraire: le roman par lettres' in *Forme et signification, essais sur les structures littéraires de Corneille à Claudel* (Paris, Corti, 1962), pp.65-103. An important discussion of the epistolary form.

25. Seylaz, J.-L., *'Les Liaisons dangereuses' et la création romanesque chez Laclos* (Geneva and Paris, Droz-Minard, 1958). One of the earliest but still one of the best studies of Laclos's creative achievement.

26. Siemek, A., *La Recherche morale et esthétique dans le roman de Crébillon fils*, Studies on Voltaire and the Eighteenth-Century, CC (Oxford, Voltaire Foundation, 1982). Probably the best monograph on the most important French novelist to portray *libertinage* before Laclos.

27. Thelander, D.R., *Laclos and the Epistolary Novel* (Geneva, Droz, 1963). A competent general survey.

28. Therrien, M., *'Les Liaisons dangereuses': une interprétation psychologique* (Paris, S.E.D.E.S., 1973). A helpful introductory guide.

29. Versini, S.L., *Laclos et la tradition, essai sur le sources et la technique des 'Liaisons dangereuses'* (Paris, Klincksieck, 1968). A monumental study situating Laclos's novel in a literary tradition.

30. ——, *Le Roman épistolaire* (Paris, Presses Universitaires de France, 1979). A general evaluation of the letter-novel.

BIBLIOGRAPHICAL SUPPLEMENT

31. Barguillet, M., '*Les Liaisons dangereuses*: commentaire de la lettre LXXXI', *Information littéraire*, XLIII, no.5 (1991), 11-16. A detailed *explication* of the famous autobiographical letter of Merteuil.

32. Byrne, P.W., '"Ces tyrans devenus mes esclaves": *Les Liaisons dangereuses* and male oppression', *Essays in French Literature*, XXXII-XXXIII (1995/1996), 1-21. Investigates master/slave imagery and the failings of the male.

33. ——, 'The moral of *Les Liaisons dangereuses*: a review of the arguments', *Essays in French Literature*, XXIII (1986), 1-18. Perceptive analysis of the morality of the tale and the varieties of hypocrisy and self-deception portrayed.

34. ——, 'The Valmont-Merteuil relationship: coming to terms with the ambiguities of Laclos's text', *Studies on Voltaire and the Eighteenth Century*, CCLXVI (Oxford, Voltaire Foundation, 1989), 373-409. Explores the existence or otherwise of genuine feelings between the major players.

35. Cazenobe, C., *Le Système du libertinage de Crébillon à Laclos*, Studies on Voltaire and the Eighteenth Century, CCLXXXII (Oxford, Voltaire Foundation, 1991). Situates Laclos in his literary context.

36. Champion, P., 'La catégorie de l'ennemi dans *Les Liaisons dangereuses*', *Poétique*, XXVI (1995), 105-23. Examination of how the idea of the enemy pervades the novel.

37. Conroy jnr, P.V., *Intimate, Intrusive and Triumphant: readers in the Liaisons dangereuses* (Amsterdam/Philadelphia, John Benjamins, 1987). An evaluation of the fictional readers in the text.

38. ——, Male bonding and female isolation in Laclos's *Les Liaisons dangereuses*', Studies on Voltaire and the Eighteenth Century, CCLXVII (Oxford, Voltaire Foundation, 1989), 253-71. Examines the general solidarity of the male characters.

39. Coulet, H., 'Analyse et sentiment dans *Les Liaisons dangereuses*' in *Le Siècle de Voltaire: hommage à René Pomeau* (Oxford, Voltaire Foundation, 1987), vol. 1, pp.305-12. An elegant essay which dissects the features stated in the title.

40. Coward, D., '*Les Liaisons dangereuses* à Londres avant la Révolution' in *Littérature et séduction: mélanges en l'honneur de Laurent Versini* (Paris, Klincksieck, 1997), pp.829-38. Demonstrates that there are few obvious responses to the novel in England despite its success in France.

41. Davies, S., 'Irish reactions to a French bestseller', *Eighteenth-Century Ireland*, XII (1997), 87-88. A note on how some Irish readers responded to the novel.

42. Delon, M., *P.-A. Choderlos de Laclos, Les Liaisons dangereuses* (Paris, Presses Universitaires de France, 1986). A well-informed and well-argued introduction to the author and his work.

43. Duranton, H., 'Laclos a-t-il lu Proust?' in *Le Siècle de Voltaire* (see *39*), pp.447-59. A stimulating comparison of the contrasting practices of the two novelists.

44. Ehrard, H., 'La société des *Liaisons dangereuses*: l'espace et le temps' in *Le Siècle de Voltaire* (see *39*), pp.461-69. An assessment of the evocation of everyday reality in the novel.

45. Fontana, B., *Politique de Laclos* (Paris, Kimé, 1996). Despite a rather misleading title, this is a spirited general introduction which deals with sexual politics and notes, in passing, the absence of fathers in the novel.

46. Herman, J., 'Miroitements intertextuels et structure métaphorique dans *Les Liaisons dangereuses*', Studies on Voltaire and the Eighteenth Century, CCLXXXXII (Oxford, Voltaire Foundation, 1991), pp.337-46. Reflections on the 'mirror' effect and the Don Juan theme.

47. Lefère, R., '*Les Liaisons dangereuses* cinématographiées: modalités d'un retour au passé' in Etudes sur le XVIIe Siècle, XXII (Bruxelles, Editions de l'Université, 1994), 137-45. Discusses the relative merits of the three film adaptations and their appeal for modern audiences.

48. Michael, C.V., 'Cécile et les dangers de l'innocence: de 'bouton de rose' à 'machine à plaisir', Studies on Voltaire and the Eighteenth Century, CCLX (1989), 323-34. Assesses the destiny of the malleable young female, berates Danceny and offers parallels with Diderot's *Supplément au voyage de Bougainville*.

49. Mortimer, A.K., 'Dialogues of the deaf: the failure of consolation in *Les Liaisons dangereuses*', Modern Language Notes III, no.IV (1996), pp.671-87. Studies the importance of 'listening' to novels.

50. O'Neal, J.C., 'The perversion of sensationism in Laclos and Sade' in *The Authority of Experience: sensationist theory in the French Enlightenment* (Pennsylvania State University Press, 1996), pp.147-70. The two authors present an 'anti-*Bildungsroman*' in their works, there is an emphasis on the destructive nature of mankind.

51. Overton, B., 'The play of letters: *Les Liaisons dangereuses* on the stage', Theatre Research International, XIII (1988), 263-74. Shrewd analysis of the problems and consequences of adapting an epistolary novel for the stage.

52. Poisson, G., *Choderlos de Laclos ou l'obstination* (Paris, Grasset, 1985). Likely to be the standard biography for many years to come.

53. Pomeau, R., *Laclos ou le paradoxe* (Paris, Hachette, 1993). A monograph which highlights the complexities and ambiguities of the novel.

54. Ray, W., 'Self-emplotment and the implication of the reader' in *Story and History: narrative authority and social identity in the eighteenth-century French and English novel* (Oxford, Blackwell, 1990), pp.319-50. A demanding chapter which questions the role of the reader and narrative authority.

55. Rosa, S., 'The anonymous public in *Les Liaisons dangereuses*' in *Studies in Eighteenth-Century Culture*, 18 (East Lansing, Colleagues Press, 1988), 479-87. While not always sure-footed, this evaluation queries the didactic function of the novel through the reactions of its own fictional readers.

56. Singerman, A.J., 'Merteuil and mirrors: Stephen Frears's Freudian reading of *Les Liaisons dangereuses*', Eighteenth-Century Fiction, V (1993), 269-81. A Freudian reading of the film which also suggests what the latter may reveal of the original.

57. Vanpée, J., 'Reading differences: the case of Letter 141 in *Les Liaisons dangereuses*', Eighteenth-Century Studies, XXVII (1993), 85-110. A discussion of gendered reading as well as a specific treatment of the stated letter.

58. Versini, L., 'Des *Liaisons dangereuses* aux liaisons farceuses', *Travaux de littérature*, VI (1993), 211-24. Highlights how the recent stage and film adaptations have brought considerable changes to the plot and language with occasionally unfortunate consequences.

59. ——, '*Les Liaisons dangereuses* à la scène et à l'écran' in *Cent ans de littérature française 1850-1950* (Paris, SEDES, 1987), pp.31-38. Investigates the early adaptations before those studied in *58*.

60. Warner, M., 'Valmont – or the Marquise Unmasked' in *The Don Giovanni Book: myths of seduction and betrayal* (London, Faber and Faber, 1990), pp.93-107. Interweaves observations on the play and film adaptations as well as the Don Juan theme with Laclos's novel.

CRITICAL GUIDES TO FRENCH TEXTS

edited by

Roger Little, Wolfgang van Emden, David Williams